Ippon!
The fight for judo's soul

To John, a fellow budoka

Chi jin yu

Dave Ham...

This book is dedicated to the memory of Paul Douglass, 4th
dan, who sadly passed away after collapsing on a judo mat.
We all live for our judo, sadly Paul died in December 2003
while practicing his. He is greatly missed.

Dave Hammond

LONDON LEAGUE PUBLICATIONS Ltd

Ippon!
The fight for judo's soul

A CIP catalogue record for this book is available from the British Library.

Published in May 2008 by:
London League Publications Ltd, P.O. Box 10441, London E14 8WR

ISBN: 978-1903659-38-0

Cover design by: Stephen McCarthy Graphic Design
                                 46, Clarence Road, London N15 5BB

Layout: Peter Lush

Printed & bound by: CPI Antony Rowe
                                 Eastbourne, Great Britain

Foreword

When I came to Britain in 1962 judo was a very different activity to what it is now. At that stage there was no weight categories and people in the West were only just getting ready to consider it as an Olympic event.

The inclusion of judo into the Olympics changed everything. The introduction of weight categories was the obvious and immediate difference, but with it came a whole new attitude to judo.

My judo is and always has been based on throwing, whatever size the opponent. I was a middleweight, so the introduction of weight categories did not affect me that much, but I did see many people, lightweight, good judo people, who until the introduction of weight categories could not compete very well. From 1964 onwards many more technically good, small people, have come to the fore in the judo world.

In fact the ideals of Pierre Coubertin, the founder of the modern Olympics, were very close to those of Doctor Jigoro Kano, the founder of Kodokan judo. Both considered that taking part in the event were of more value than any prizes given out at the end.

In judo the scoring system was changed around the same time as the introduction of weight categories and again on the face of it, this was a progressive move. In my time it was *ippon* and *wazari* and that was it. The introduction of the smaller scores of *yuko* and *koka* was aimed at rewarding those that put in attacks, even if they did not result in a big throw.

The problem was and this remains the case, is, the British especially, went in for *koka*-training. They were not trying to throw for a proper *ippon*, they were grabbing legs and so on, doing anything that would give them a minor score to hold onto. I recall facing a training partner that was only intent on grabbing my leg. I simply didn't understand what he was trying to do. I said: "What are you doing," he said, "Oh, this is *koka*-training." Still people in the British Judo Association do this type of training. Those young people that I met are now national coaches.

British judo has been stumped by this and finds itself 40 years behind the progress that has been made in Japan. Grip-fighting and the desire to avoid throws has degenerated much of modern British judo.

I believe it is important that those of us who instruct judo return to the teaching of *ippon* judo. We must teach the judo spirit of going all-out for the big throws. You must try for the *ippon* score. Training for *koka* scores has pushed *ippon* judo out. In Japan, even though the *koka* score is valid there, they still train for the *ippon*. That is what we must aim to do here as well.

When I arrived in Britain there were a lot of people practicing judo. Now the numbers are smaller. I think this is because here there is not a proper way of training. People are either fast-tracked into competitive judo, or they become disenchanted and move quickly to other things. The problem lies in the coaching methods. Too few coaches teach proper *ippon* judo. Good judo lasts much longer than if you train for the low scores and of course, you can improve, slowly but surely. I believe that it is still possible to train a child with proper *ippon* judo so that they could be good enough to compete at Olympic level, but nobody is aiming to do that in Britain.

Outside of judo in Britain, it is clearly understood that there needs to be a balance between academic study and physical sport. This too is an essential aspect of Kano's Kodokan *judo*. Some people do a little bit of Judo and hard studies, some fifty-fifty and help each other. Some, like me, stopped studying and did judo too much. That is no good. Kano's idea was about the balance and that is what it should be about. That remains the Kodokan way and I am pleased to say that is the way that judo is approached by the British Judo Council. They call their way of looking at judo *kyu-shin-do*. To me, *kyu-shin-do* equals Kodokan judo. Too many people miss the philosophical side of judo because they want to take the short cut to championship success. It is deeply ironic, then that Kodokan Judo has a philosophy which fits neatly with those of the Olympic Games.

Kodokan Judo philosophy and IJF philosophy do not go together, however. IJF philosophy is all about winning, nothing else. British judo too is about how to win. The way that people try to debase judo in order to win continues. Currently if you examine a modern contest judo suit and compare it to what was worn when I was young the thickness of the material is immediately evident. These thick suits were designed to stop your partner getting a good grip – another way of trying to hedge your bets. It suited big westerners to have these kits when fighting smaller Japanese, who struggled to hold such thick collars.

For me judo remains a wonderful activity. My competitive days have long passed, but I now try to teach both good quality judo and judo philosophy as handed down by Doctor Jigoro Kano.

The challenge for the judo authorities of the world is to stop the decline in interest in our art. For that it must become again what Doctor Kano wanted it to be: an art for all, one that helps develop the individual both physically and mentally.

Akinori Hosaka (Kodokan Hachidan)

Akinori Hosaka, 8th *dan*, is the highest graded Kodokan man resident in Britain. A former All-Japan competitor, he has coached to Olympic level. Now he sees his role as promoting traditional judo and its values.

About the author

Dave Hammond has been practising and study judo since 1982. He first took up the art seeing it as a means of self-defence, but quickly encompassed its other attributes. He has competed at national level with the British Judo Association, the British Judo Council and *Seishin Budo*. He attained his first dan in 2000. Also graded in *tomiki aikido*, he is a qualified instructor who has taught self-defence and transferable judo skills to professional rugby players. He currently runs his own judo club in Dundee, Scotland.

He is also a professional writer whose work on judo in particular and sport in general has been published by a variety of publications including *The Times*, *The Sunday Times*, *The Herald*, *Four four Two* and *Rugby News*. He has been editor of *Judoka*, the national magazine of the British Judo Council since 2000.

This book is written by Dave Hammond in a personal capacity, and does not necessarily represent the views of the British Judo Council.

Previous books by Dave Hammond:

Foul Play: A Class analysis of sport
The Club: Life and times of Blackheath FC
Blackheath FC in pictures.

He was also the authenticator for the Little Gem Collins book on Basketball.

Introduction

In 2007 the British Judo Association, under the guidance of its technical coach, the Russian Andrew Moshanov, banned certain dangerous techniques from junior judo competition.

The techniques in question were sacrifice techniques, headed up by drop-seoinage, which had been the staple diet of contest judo for decades.

The reasoning behind the ban was not new. Drop-seoinage had been despised by judo traditionalists for generations. The long-term damage to the knees of *tori* (the thrower) was often cited by coaches as its biggest problem. Yet the problems posed by drop-seoinage go much deeper than a willingness of an individual to suffer long-term damage in search of short-term gain. The receiver of the technique is always in danger of receiving neck and shoulder injuries and as our culture moves inexorably towards a litigation society the implications for judo were becoming increasingly ominous.

The problem that judo authorities faced over drop-seoinage is one that encapsulates the divide between traditionalists and modernizers. The irony is that the ban was introduced by modernizers who have had to accept the wisdom of a more traditional approach.

Fear for the safety of *uki* (the receiver of the throw) is only one aspect of the British Judo Association's experimental ban on sacrifice techniques. It has, somewhat belatedly, become clear that over-emphasis on a throw that requires limited learning time is detrimental to further judo progress. Those brought up on an early diet of sacrifice techniques struggle to stay on their feet and think of more commanding standing judo. As those at a high level learn to counter the drop the overall ability of their exponents become exposed. The medals dry up.

Overall the development of drop-seoinage has cost British Judo dearly in many ways. The lack of Olympic success, the injury to practitioners at every level and the resulting drop in attendance at club level cannot be put down solely to one technique, but it would be difficult to over-emphasis just how bad for judo as a whole drop-seoinage has been.

Moshanov knows that for judo to be successful again, coaches must return to teaching fundamental principles of the art. They must return to the core techniques that were taught across the world in the 1950s and 1960s if they are to nurture competent long-term judo practitioners. Once these basics are mastered it becomes easier for an exponent to move on to more complex techniques.

Moshanov, as technical director, has more on his mind than simple medal success. For an elite to emerge, there must be a strong base in the first place and the task for all judo associations currently is to source and retain members at club level. This will be no mean feat and it will not be achieved without attention to detail.

This short book is basically historical. Yet I believe the purpose of memory is to look forward, not backwards. It is not a case of reminiscing; it is of seeing how we arrived at where we are and considering how we can move forward. If judo is to remain anything like as popular an activity as it currently is, it must learn the lessons of its own history.

Dave Hammond

Dundee

April 2008

The much-debated drop knee *seoinage*. This technique is now banned in junior contests. It can easily result in injury to both parties. It does not fit into judo as a martial art and is seen by traditionalists as a sloppy way of taking an opponent to the mat.

Acknowledgements

It is customary to thank a number of people for the assistance, support and encouragement given in the production of a book and as a traditionalist I see no reason to do any different.

My first debt of gratitude goes to Allan Jones, formerly of the British Judo Council, now with Seishin Budo. It was as a pupil of Allan's that I was alerted to the fact that judo was such a many faceted activity. Over the years many people have inadvertently helped me with this book by training with me, it would be impossible to name them all. I would, however like to make special mention of a number of people who have guided my judo thoughts: Mr. G. R (Jim) Mealing, 7th *dan*, George Temperton, 5th dan have both enlightened me on various aspect of my chosen art and John Barton, 3rd *dan* has spent many an hour in thoughtful discussion with me. Stuart Gordon, 2nd *dan*, was an outstanding *kata* partner.

Peter Baldwin and Charlie Clark were responsible for progressing my judo skills during my time in south east London. Mark Arbuthnott of Brechin *Mudanshakai* must be thanked for reading the manuscript and making significant suggestions and special thanks should also be afforded the members of the *Budo Shin Ryu* judo club in Newcastle for allowing one of their weekly training sessions to be turned into a photo shoot for this book. During that session Phill Dobson, 2nd *kyu* took charge of the camera while Dave Wright, 3rd *dan* and Steve George, 1st *dan* performed willingly as photo-fodder.

My wife, Jacqui should be thanked for her patience as I travelled the country attending various courses, for the evenings I spend in the *dojo* instead of at home, and for encouraging me to return to the mat after injury had finished my fighting career.

I would also like to thank Peter Lush and Dave Farrar of London League Publications Ltd for agreeing to publish the book, Steve McCarthy for designing the cover, and the staff of Antony Rowe Ltd for printing it.

Photographs

The photographs demonstrating judo are by Phill Dobson, others are from private collections unless otherwise credited. No copyright has been intentionally breached; please contact London League Publications Ltd if you believe there has been a breach of copyright.

Contents

Glossary

Ashi-garami: leg entanglement
Atemi: striking
Dojo: judo training hall
Dan: master grade, black belt.
Goshin jutsu: the Kodokan's self-defence system encapsulated in a 21 technique *kata*
Ippon: winning score, 10 points.
Judo: the gentle, or supple way
Judoka: someone who practices judo. In Japan this usually refers to somebody of a high grade.
Kata: prearranged forms.
Koka: score of three points
Katsu: resuscitation techniques
Kyu: pupil grade. Anything under *dan* grade

Matte: stop
Nage: throw
Newaza: ground techniques
Randori: free practice
Rei: bow
Ryu: School or system.
Sensei: teacher, instructor.
Seoinage: shoulder throw
Shiai: contest
Shodan: first *dan*.
Tori: person executing technique.
Tsukuri: breaking of balance
Uke: person receiving technique
Waza: technique
Wazari: seven points
Yuko: five points

1. Koka
Kano's bright idea

As with other human activities, sport has changed over the centuries. Man has been 'playing' ever since he has had spare time on his hands – and probably even before then. Most of the major sports of the 21st century have their roots so far back in time that the exact origins are unclear. Football is *the* global sport and while it is easy to identify the beginning of association football as an organised field sport, it is not quite so easy to talk about its exact genesis.

What is clear is that all field invasion games are a reflection of the values of humanity and as such continue to have a militaristic undertone. Most Olympic individual sports too have a martial background, even though that genesis has been lost in time. Archery's origins as a combat art are clear, but hammer throwing and javelin, for instance, also owe their origins to military skills.

Of the world's most popular sports, judo and basketball are the latecomers. Basketball was devised in 1884 by a Dr James Naismith who, by inventing his game, was solving a very particular problem. Dr Naismith was of the muscular Christian school of thought and at the Massachusetts School for Christian Workers in Springfield, was responsible for the physical recreation of budding young missionaries. A child of his time, who was keen on rugby, Naismith wanted a robust team invasion sport but was limited by the facilities at his disposal and the number of young men under his charge. Basketball, then, was born as a completely new sport, and one which reflected the values of Naismith and the society in which he operated.

Two years earlier in Tokyo, Japan, Jigoro Kano was establishing his new 'sport', Kodokan judo. On the face of it, Kano's development did not fit the same profile as Naismith's. Naismith supposedly started from scratch, whereas Kano had a wealth of experience in other jujutsu to draw from as he put together his variation of those skills. He was the recognised head of two jujutsu styles, the *Kito Ryu* and *Tenshin Shin'Yo Ryu*. He had studied and continued to study fighting arts from around the world and in effect he plagiarised with gay abandon.

1

The term jujutsu incorporated a number of earlier Japanese fighting arts and in synthesising Kodokan judo from those arts Kano was establishing another jutsu, albeit one which had a sporting element to it. Kodokan judo was, therefore, fundamentally a jutsu, a fact that Kano was only too willing to acknowledge.

The fundamental difference between Kano and Naismith, however, is that what Kano was not and never had been studying was sport. In his later life, Kano was recognised as a champion of sport; he was Asia's first representative on the Olympic Committee, but when it came to judo, his very own invention, he considered what he was developing to be far beyond a mere sport. Like Naismith, he too, was a child of his time. The difference was that Kano's Japan was at a very, very different stage of its development than Naismith's America.

Jigoro Kano was born in 1860, in Mikage, a small coastal village. At that time Japan was going through significant cultural and economic change. The feudalism that his father, an educated man, had known was on the way out. Western influences, carried by trade and commerce were on their way in. Kano was a sharp young man and he understood the implications of westernisation in Japan. Largely, despite his patriotic attitude, he accepted the western influences recognising that Japan had to move with the time and assimilate other cultures if it was to be a player on the world stage.

The young Jigoro received much of his early education from his father but when he was just nine years old his mother died and the family moved to Tokyo, the new capital of Japan, where he attended school.

Tokyo was an uncertain place to live in the late 1860s and early 1870s. The samurai classes were, in effect, disbanded, leaving a large number of men, trained in the martial arts, without direction. Used to carrying their arms openly, they were finally banned from carrying swords around the time that the Kano family arrived in the capital.

The social unrest would undoubtedly have affected the young Jigoro. A physically weak boy, he was acutely aware of his social surroundings. He was also aware that, physically, he was not in a position to defend himself from the local bullies. A bright boy who excelled at school, he was despised by many who did not reach his academic heights. In short, he was what in later generations would be termed a 'geek'.

On his arrival at his new school Kano attempted to ingratiate himself and at the same time improve his physique by playing games such as baseball, but he also attempted to seek out somebody to give him martial arts training.

In his quest to find an instructor he was discouraged and initially thwarted. The martial arts had become somewhat of an anachronism in modern Japan. The old samurai were discredited and the new capitalist culture had no place for either these fighting men or their ancient arts. Kano approached three masters of various jujutsu asking for tuition and was rejected each time, with his father's advice to get involved in modern sports ringing in his ears.

Nevertheless Kano persisted and in 1877 finally found a martial arts instructor willing to teach him. *Tenshin Shin'yo Ryu* emphasised *atemi waza*, striking techniques, and grappling and Kano quickly became adept. Ever the scholar, even at this early stage, he was very keen to understand the mechanics of the techniques of *Tenshin Shin'yo*: he didn't just want his techniques to work, he wanted to know every how and why.

On the death of his *Tenshin Shin'yo* instructor in 1881, Kano took up another jutsu, that of the *Kito Ryu* school. As is the case with the variety of jujutsu that still exist to this day, the differences between various schools was immense. Under the banner of *Kito Ryu*, a school with a considerably older tradition than that of *Tenshin Shin'yo*, Kano was exposed to a greater number of *nagewaza* - throwing - techniques. He was also initiated into a far subtler, more philosophical, attitude to the art he was learning.

The jujutsu arts were a part of Japanese culture that traced back to feudal times. There were many ryu, but in truth, far fewer broad styles. Many kept their techniques secret to give them an advantage on the field of battle. Yet while it may seem there are many forms of martial arts, they all have basic tenets to work from, whatever their origins or the peculiarities of individual instructors: there may be a relatively large number of ways that even now a judo or jujutsu instructor can demonstrate *shimewaza* - strangles - but the fact is that there are only four attacks on the neck: those that stop the blood supply to the brain, those that stop the air supply, those that break the neck and the rather more esoteric act of attacking a pressure point.

These skills were taught to the Japanese equivalent of western medieval knights. What went with them was also something similar to the knightly code of honour. Samurai were taught that their art, the art of warfare, was an honourable one. They learned a chivalric code and were given a spiritual understanding of their calling. *Bushido* was the generic term for the guiding principles that shaped Japan's warrior elite.

The need for these skills more or less died out with the end of the protracted civil wars that Japan had been subject to, which ceased at the beginning of the Edo period in 1603. As in the west, however, the skills and the codes that had been developed for war where not jettisoned, but adapted for the new conditions and a different clientele. The emphasis switched from the practicalities of battlefield skills to the self-development of the individual. That is not to say, however, that the specific combat skills were necessarily neutered.

By the early 19th century, jujutsu was being taught to a much changed audience. It had been absorbed into a wider Japanese culture. It did, however, retain a certain level of mystery with the number of varying schools remaining high. The tradition was that when an individual had mastered his art, he would often breakaway from his original *sensei* – teacher - to develop his own version of what he had been taught. Pupils of Morihei Uyeshiba, the founder of aikido followed this path, so that today there are a number of different aikido styles, frequently named after their originators, who themselves were taught by Uyeshiba.

There also remains a number of jujutsu and karate instructors that have made similar breaks, not all of them realising that they may have developed idiosyncrasies to their style that suit them, but are not necessarily easily absorbed by others: the point of establishing your own school should be to develop your pupils, rather than merely show off what you can do.

By the time Jigoro Kano set out on his quest for a master to teach him, jujutsu had been pushed far away from its esteemed origins. It was taught at times almost furtively in places and to people and for reasons that could be described as dubious.

Yet enough of the original codes remained that it was not totally swept into the back alleys of Tokyo. The early masters that Kano approached may not have been keen to teach the youngster, but there was no shame in what they knew. Nor was it merely their fighting skills that were sought out. As part of their training, many became expert bonesetters and often they could be found plying their trade as osteopaths. It is a tradition that lasted well into the days of Kodokan judo, with bone setting being an art that was associated with high-graded *judoka* even after the Second World War.

Kano had come to the jutsu arts for the simple reason of wishing to learn a self-defence system. He would not be the first or last to enter a *dojo* with such a specific aim that got lost somewhere on the path to mastering a martial art.

By the time he was ready to establish his own school of martial arts, Kano had already made a significant personal journey. He could, of course, have simply opened up a *dojo* teaching *Tenshin Shin'yo* or *Kito Ryu* jujutsu, or both, or even a combination of the two. He was by that time a recognised master of both, but Kano clearly saw that if the martial arts were to continue at all into the 20th century they needed a major overhaul.

It is not that Kano managed to synthesise his Kodokan judo from a number of martial arts that was his genius. The real key to ensuring that Kodokan judo outstripped every martial art that went before it, and in a very real way helped some of the others even to survive, was placing it squarely in a cultural setting that was acceptable to the emerging, westernised Japan. Judo may have been built on the traditions of ancient Japan, but it was also devised with an eye to the future.

Kano made this clear in 1880: "The world is changing, and jujutsu has to change too," he said. "I don't think it's practical to limit ourselves to one particular style. I no longer see any point in keeping the techniques of each jujutsu school secret. It would be better to experiment with a whole range of techniques and select the ones you want to use, changing them if necessary."

Already the idea of developing a new art altogether was growing in Kano's mind. Techniques were plundered, not just from the jujutsu that Kano had mastered, but from fighting arts around the world. Kano studied western boxing and wrestling. It was from the latter that it is said he devised *kata-garuma*, the shoulder wheel that he used so effectively to despatch a considerably bigger opponent. The legend has it that Kano had been having trouble contesting with a larger training partner and came across a *kata-garuma* style technique in a wrestling book. The story is possibly apocryphal, but certainly Kano did take the opportunity to study western arts on his travels abroad and as an educationalist his willingness to study books was evident.

Kano managed to virtually invent other techniques because of the systematic way he studied the fighting arts. One of his early pupils, the feted Shiro Saigo had learnt how to step off of Kano's hip technique, so the master developed *harai-goshi*, the sweeping loin throw that catches *uke* as he comes round the hips.

The concept at the core of Kano's techniques was not new. The 'ju' in jujutsu was a clear indication that long before Kano, the idea of using another's force and momentum against them was well established. What was new, however, was that Kano understood and explained clearly the need to break balance – the use of *kuzushi*. This was somewhat of a Newtonian event. Just as Isaac Newton did not invent gravity, but understood and explained it, the better to harness it, thus Kano enlightened fighters as to why their techniques worked. His observations regarding *kuzushi* ensured that all the techniques he incorporated into judo had to be proven as workable.

From the very outset, however, Kano intended his art to be something more than a new, improved, or even amalgamated jujutsu. He founded his first martial arts school in 1882 and in an opening speech to his pupils gathered before him, he made it clear that a new beginning had been made: "I want you all to listen carefully to what I have to say," he began solemnly. "Jujutsu training is more than just physical exercise. It should promote mental discipline and moral virtue as well. But we live in an era when jujutsu masters are squaring off against sumo wrestlers for entertainment's sake and performing music halls for money. Bullies are using jujutsu to intimidate people. Jujutsu has

6

fallen into disrepute. Little attention is paid to proper training and teaching methods, and students are injured needlessly. Under the circumstances, jujutsu isn't attracting the right kind of following.

"Nowadays few men of good character would pursue an interest in jujutsu for long. Those who do are generally roughnecks, men who are fond of fighting or who don't have enough mental discipline to get an education. My own belief is that jujutsu training should improve a man's character as well as his physical powers.

"The ideal should be to prevent fights, to promote education, and to cultivate good manners and civilised behaviour. From today we will no longer practise jujutsu. We will practise something new, which we will call judo."

The adding of the 'do' to the end of the term was no accident. Kano, despite his youth and lack of formal standing, was confident enough to make a clear break with the past. Forever the educator, he was stating clearly that his art was as much about the personal development of his pupils as it was about their fighting prowess.

It was a luxury that he could afford for the simplest of reasons: Kodokan judo was, as a fighting art, superior to what had gone before.

Proof of that was to come soon enough and with devastating effect. But in the meantime Kano had to establish the clear distinction between what he was currently doing and what had gone before.

He did this in a number of novel ways, the ranking system that he introduced being of significance here. Up until Kodokan judo, there was no ranking system in jujutsu. Progression may or may not have been noted with certificates, but the belt system was something altogether different. Kano did not devise the multicolour belt system, that came later via Kawaishi, who was based in France at the time, but he did divide his pupils into *kyu* and *dan* grades. Students had to progress through a number of *kyu*, pupil, grades before they could wear a black belt and be considered a dan, master, grade. Initially Kano devised a system that incorporated three *kyu* and three *dan* grades.

There are a number of myths surrounding this system. It did not come from the old martial arts schools that would have seen little point in it. The issuing of coloured belts came later, but in the first instance, within a year of establishing the Kodokan, Kano had bestowed the rank of *shodan* on his two top, and indeed original students, Saigo and Tsunejiro Tomita.

Saigo, incidentally, left the Kodokan under a cloud, having been involved in a street brawl that saw him picked up by the police. A number of officers were injured in the ensuing melee and in hearing of the incident Kano, no doubt with a heavy heart, banished his former pupil. Some sort of rehabilitation of Saigo was established on his death – he was posthumously promoted to sixth *dan*.

Today some see the *dan* grade as signifying the holder as an expert, or master, while others suggest that the awarding of a black belt signifies nothing other than the holder is ready to start his or her training in earnest. The truth is a hybrid of these two views.

Certainly, Kano did not give Saigo or Tomita *dan* grades because he thought these two, who were already highly accomplished martial artists, were only just ready to have the secrets of judo opened up to them. Both had helped Kano with the development of judo techniques, so such a perspective would have been an insult.

The term *shodan* does suggest some sort of beginning, but the suffix dan, denotes a mastery of some sort.

From the beginning, the switch from *kyu* grade to *dan* has always been a significant one. Syllabuses may vary across the globe and through time, but the awarding of a *dan* grade and the coveted black belt that goes with it always implies that the holder has a certain mastery.

If judo was to be nothing but a fighting art, the ranking system would make no sense at all. Senior *dan* grades are achieved only after a practitioner has past his fighting prime and that has been the case since the early days. Equally if, as some modern judo exponents suggest, judo was devised as a combat sport, the grading system would be illogical. Ranking would mean little, if anything, and logically a fighter should move down the grades as his career wanes. This is the case with sumo. The truth is that Kano saw, from day one, that his art was to be neither a sport nor merely a fighting art.

As well as instigating a ranking system, Kano also established a clear way of training for his students. *Randori* - free fighting - was not entirely new, but it was a difficult practice with many *ryu*. Kano saw huge advantages in *randori*. It was a means of testing the efficacy of certain skills and it gave the opportunity to test the fighting spirit of his trainees. The problem that nobody seemed to have solved before Kano was how to make *randori* safe without completely castrating it.

Some of the pre-Kodokan jujutsu schools concentrated on *kata*, the choreographed movement of attack and defence as a means of getting round this problem; others suffered the loss of adherents to injury. Kano analysed the problem and after accepting that *randori*, via the actual seizing of a training partner's apparel was the key, systematically removed techniques that did not fit in with such training.

Kano made it clear that *randori* was the most essential element to the training of judo. It is only through *randori* that an individual can develop a fighting spirit. *Atemi* was removed from regular training not because of a lack of efficacy, but as Kano clearly pointed out because it was dangerous to keep it in.

He did not, however, have any intentions of throwing the baby out with the bath water. Some techniques that Kano excluded from *randori* were absorbed into *katas*, others were taught separately. Neck locks, wristlocks and leg locks are all part of judo as are strikes with the elbows, hands and feet. Devastating attacks on pressure points are also part of the canon of judo.

There is another reason why the more lethal aspects of judo are not part of *randori*. Because Kano intended his art to be a moral, physical and intellectual learning process open to all, students would not become exposed to the more deadly aspects until they had gone a certain way down that learning path. To this day there are many that claim to be experts at judo who know little or nothing beyond the mat craft required to win tournaments. It is unlikely that Kano would have bestowed any great rank upon these people.

They would have been, as far as Kano was concerned at stage two of a three stage development. Stage one, according to Kano was the learning of basic judo techniques and self-defence skills. Stage two incorporated a greater physical ability to match mind and body and to absorb lessons and pass them on. The highest level of judo development was to make use of the skills acquired through judo to make a contribution to society, not just in judo, but in every day life – in short Kano was in the business of character development.

Kano summed up his attitude to judo in relation to what went before thus: "Although Kodokan judo begins with the *randori* and the *kata*, unlike jujutsu, it is based on the principles of physical education and lays stress on the harmonious development of body and muscles. The principle described as the way to use body and mind most efficiently is indeed the great principle of humanity. It is a moral doctrine." (quoted in *Judo: a sport and a way of life*, published by the IJF, 1999.)

If Kano was trying to bring a more modern outlook to martial arts, there is no evidence, either from the time of the establishment of the Kodokan, nor later, that he had in mind a sport as we know by today's terms. Sporting elements were introduced to judo for very sound reasons, but it is clear that Kano did not see judo as a sport, despite the fact that he was very keen on developing Japanese interest in western sports. He was Asia's first representative on the Olympic Committee, but even then there is no evidence to suggest that he wished judo to be considered for Olympic sport status, as we shall learn later.

For Kano, his art was a huge learning tool for life, one that could be used by young and old alike, one that had no losers, one where its participants grew as individuals and assisted with the development of others along the way: mutual welfare and benefit was to be one his great mantras.

Contest, or *shiai*, to use the Japanese term, has always been an integral part of Judo, but Kano recognised that the key element to making Judo a means of personal improvement was neither *shiai* nor *kata*: *randori* was to be the activity that both marked judo as being a superior form of martial art and as a means of an individual constantly testing himself in a controlled and therefore safe environment.

He established the first of his Red versus White annual contests in 1884, an event that remains at the core of Kodokan judo and is, in fact, the longest running sporting event in the

Atemi waza (striking techniques) have always been part of judo.
The *kime-no-kata* demonstrates a blow to the testicles
after an attacker from the rear has been thrown.

world. These contest have always held significance in terms of the Kodokan's pecking order, but just as significant as those annual contests was the establishment, around the same time, of the *kangeiko* training period, a severe mid-winter session that the Kodokan still use today, whereby training starts very early in the morning and continues in a cold dojo for a number of hours. This continues for a period of 10 days and is seen as part of the building of character and strength of spirit that Kano desired from his students. The summer equivalent of the *kangeiko*, the *shochugeiko*, was not established until 1896.

Kano made it very clear that whilst he owed much to his jujutsu past, he was also trying to establish something that had a completely different ethical start point, as he explained in 1898: "Of course I teach 'jutsu'," he confessed. "But it is upon 'do,' 'way' or 'principle' that I want to lay special stress. The Kodokan judo I teach has wider aims and differs in techniques. There are two other reasons why I avoided the term jujutsu. One is that there were jujutsu schools which often indulged in violent and dangerous techniques in throwing or twisting arms and legs. Seeing these things, many people had come to believe that jujutsu was harmful. Again, in an exercise hall where supervision was inadequate, the senior pupils would wantonly throw down the juniors or pick quarrels, so that jujutsu was despised. I wished to show that what I taught was not a dangerous thing and would not needlessly injure any person.

"Some jujutsu masters made their living by organising troupes and putting on exhibition matches. Others went so far as to stage bouts between professional sumo wrestlers and jujutsu men. Such degrading practices of prostituting martial arts were repugnant to me, so I avoided the term jujutsu." It would be interesting to know what Kano's reaction to judo people being involved in mixed martial arts would be.

Nevertheless, it was a very high profile contest that set Kodokan judo on the path of eclipsing all the grappling arts that went before it. In 1888, or according to some accounts 1886, The Tokyo Police were casting around for an unarmed fighting system for their officers. Naturally a number of *ryu* were interested in taking this on, so it was agreed that a contest should decide which school would get the contract. In terms of the future of the arts concerned this contest was very much a do or die.

There were virtually no rules and no time limits. Submission or, in effect, knock-out was the aim and brutality was the game. That battle is now shrouded in myth. Were there 12 or 15 bouts? Did the Kodokan lose any? Did any deaths or permanent injuries occur?

What is not disputed is that some gruelling and intense contests were fought and that the overall conclusion was that Kano's modernised, scientific approach to unarmed combat was the outright victor. As far as he had travelled down the road of judo being an holistic activity that benefited mind, body and soul, the founder had not forgotten the original tenant: "The thorough study of defence against attack is the foundation and the ability to train the body and cultivate the mind come from this study [of judo]."

Thanks to Kano the ideology behind jujutsu was being completely converted to judo. There remained, and remain, a number of jujutsu forms outside judo, but the driving force from then on was the acceptance that the study of martial arts was as much a personal journey as it was a fighting art: it was now not important to be the best, but instead be the best one could be. Through the study of the art, an individual develops as a person.

All modern martial artists should be grateful for Kano's establishment of that ethos. Without it modern karate or *aikido* would not exist. Kano successfully brought these arts out of the backstreets and made it acceptable to train in them.

If he had not won such wide acceptance, schools and municipal halls would not welcome men and women in strange white clothing, learning what appears to be a systemised method of brutality. Jujutsu would have remained a dark secret, studied by numbers comparable to English Cornish wrestling, or at best a quirky hobby such as studying fighting with broadswords.

The importance of individual development through judo can be seen by the grading system. Despite the change of emphasis that has seen judo morph into an Olympic sport, the grading system still rewards *judoka* with further dan grades when long past their fighting peak. Individuals develop a clearer understanding of their art, they study the more esoteric aspects of judo, such as *katas*, *katsu* (now replaced in most syllabuses by first aid), teaching methods and the non-*randori* applications of judo. Even as late as the end of the 20th century, former world champion Graeme Randall admitted to the author that he would be a better *judoka* once he finished his fighting career.

In fact Kano's progress from a jujutsu tyro to master of a way, or 'do' was one that has been followed by thousands of martial artists since, who have entered a *dojo* with the express intention of learning a practical self-defence system before gradually being initiated into a world of self-development, coming out the other side as a more balanced individual, at one with themselves and ready to pass on their skills and knowledge to the next generation. Each step, including the attainment of the coveted black belt, simply leads to a thirst for more enlightenment, a deeper understanding of the art and oneself.

It is perhaps over-emphasised how low the old jujutsu schools had gone in Japanese eyes. With the onrush of western ideas, there was still a residue of pride in the arts of Japan's past, including the fighting spirit of the samurai codes of honour and the *budo* creed. In 1895 the *Dai Nippon Butokukai* (DNBK) was established to promote *Bushido* (the way of the warrior). The Butokukai was set up under the authority of the Ministry of Education, aiming to set standards, issue licences and oversee the development of the martial ways generally. This would not have been possible if *budo* was as widely despised as many historians believe. With the aid of Kano, the *budo* ethos and dedication to martial skills was re-introduced to mainstream Japanese culture. It would soon travel the world.

The DNBK became famed as a place that produced martial artists of the highest quality, not just in judo. Kendo was one of the key activities at the Butokukai, as was swimming. In judo terms there was naturally a cross-over with the by-then well-established Kodokan. One of the key judo instructors at the Butokukai was Hajimi Isogai, who had entered the Kodokan in 1891. At the Butokukai, Isogai helped produce two of the most famous pioneers of judo in Europe, Kenshiro Abbe, who formed the British Judo Council and Abbe's *kata* partner, Haku Michigami, who had a great influence on French judo. Isogai himself earned his 10th *dan* in 1937, 10 years before his death, being awarded the accolade by Kano just before the latter's death.

Kodokan judo's absorption into Japanese culture was achieved in remarkably quick time. It hinged on old, well respected samurai traditions, yet its alignment with a more modern and western approach was ideal for the time. There was enough of the old and the new to appease all. Kano proved very quickly that his fighting system was both effective, yet controlled just enough to be acceptable to the modernisers. His standing in Japanese society was such that he could promote his art well and with the support of those in high places. Judo was about to become part of the fabric of modern Japanese living. Just like western traditions that had been invented or modified in the Victorian era, judo embedded itself into society and appeared to have been there forever. It was as if with the changes the Japanese endured, they could take something from the past and say proudly: 'this is timeless and Japanese. It fits with the modern world and proves that we have a cultural heritage to show off to the rest of the world.' And they were right.

2. Yuko
Judo's children: Sambo and Brazilian jujutsu

By the turn of the century Kodokan judo had something in the region of 5,000 practitioners. It was an incredible step from the nine students that had enrolled in the Kodokan's first year and the eight that promised to train under Kano initially in 1882. The growth of the art was partially down to its efficacy, but also due to the position of respect and authority that Kano had established for himself in the wider world.

Kano had graduated from Tokyo University in 1881 and immediately gone into higher education. In 1889, at the request of the Japanese Imperial Household he embarked on a journey to Europe to study European educational institutions. His work was not completed until January 1891, by which time Kano had absorbed much about European culture.

He also continued to be responsive to innovations around the development of judo, soaking up lessons from other fighting systems. He was certainly not ashamed of plagiarising.

Neither was he afraid to take on board the suggestions of others, acknowledging their input as he did so. In 1906 he gathered together a Council of Masters to help formulate the judo *katas*. The flow of information went against the grain of former jujutsu masters, but by this time Kano's position at the head of Japanese martial arts was unassailable.

Originally he had been asked by the Butokukai to develop a series of *katas*, but on reflection thought that better results would be achieved if he assembled the countries leading martial artists to discuss the matter. He therefore brought together a committee of 18 masters to devise a series of *katas* that would involve both defence and attack.

Kano took the idea of development through *kata* even further, however. The committee agreed the development of the *nage-no-kata* and with some debate *kime-no-kata* and *the katami-no-kata*, completing the *randori-no-kata*, but there was no agreement on the *ju-no-kata*, which Kano had already established at the Kodokan. The Butokukai, instead developed its own *ju-no-kata*.

More significantly, however, Kano continued to develop *kata* as something more than the learning of self-defence or Judo *randori* moves. He started work on the *itsutsu kata* around 1897, admitting that it had nothing to do with either martial arts or sport. He said: "In the jujutsu of the past, the purpose of all forms of exercise was, either directly or indirectly, to attack or defend against attack. However the *itsutsu no kata* express natural energy through movement and have no relationship to attack or defence at all. I would like to create many of these kinds of *kata* with the purpose of developing an aesthetic sentiment through movement or various postures while at the same time training the body. When these new types of *kata* are perfected we will have realised something that can be called 'national physical education."

Kodokan judo continued to learn lessons. Apart from the gathering of Masters for the establishment of the Judo-no-Kata, Kano most notably revised his attitude to groundwork within judo after his students had received a beating in a match against the *Fusen Ryu* jujutsu school. The *Fusen Ryu* people out-grappled the *Kodokan* exponents on the ground after getting there in a somewhat messy style. Kano then asked the *Fusen* Master, Mataemon Tanabe to instruct him in *newaza* - ground fighting techniques. He also studied the grappling techniques of yet another groundwork system before further embedding *newaza* into his judo system.

Kano did not want judo to become a ground-based art however and the rules, which Kano changed in 1925 to preserve the ascendancy of *tachiwaza*, or standing techniques, were couched to ensure that before contestants moved into ground work a certain proficiency is seen in *tachiwaza* first.

Kano believed that groundwork skills were easier to pick up than those of standing techniques. More importantly he could see that if groundwork was allowed ascendancy over *tachiwaza*, people would train in drag-down techniques to get onto the floor, rather than persevering with attempts to perfect their throws. In this he was pre-empting a debate that re-emerged once judo was an internationally recognised sport with Olympic status. Further rule changes were required long after Kano's death to combat the unseemly attempts of *newaza* specialist to make rapid progress onto the floor in contest.

The fact that a number of matches between Kodokan judo and other jujutsu exponents were arranged in these early days should not be seen as an indication that judo or any of the other jujutsu were at this stage transforming into sports. The contests were fought for the purpose of establishing which art was the most efficient. In itself this may seem puerile, yet it is an argument that continues to this day. Many will claim their own arts as being the most effective for varying reasons, when the truth is that most fighting systems that have been developed over years are workable.

Judo's superiority was, as we have seen, largely down to the fact that Kano plagiarised. He also systemised his training methods and approached the art in a far more scientific manner than those that attempted to compete with him.

Contest also had to be an integral part of judo for other reasons, however. As we have seen, the inclusion of free-fighting gave judo practitioners an edge over those that did not use such a training method. For those who competed against each other at judo there was also the very real addition of the contest being another aspect of their own personal development. For those who find it initially difficult, the steeling of one-self to take on another in physical combat can be an uplifting experience, one that has a very real effect on the development of self-confidence. This has implications not just in a physical confrontation situation, which most people wish to avoid, but in the way that individuals interact with others socially and in the workplace.

Kano always had grand ideas for the development of his fighting system. His career within education gave him the perfect vehicle to promote judo as an activity that was appropriate to be taught in schools. He had, as we have seen, been overseas to study European education methods in 1899 and after his return he played a significant part in the development of the Japanese education system, being attached to the Ministry of Education in a number of roles.

Naturally he did not pass up the opportunity to promote judo across the board. He was, however, assisted by the nature of the activity that he had created. As a form of general fitness exercise judo was and remains an excellent tool for learning. The philosophies that Kano had attached to judo made it easy to sell to those concerned with education. Body management and physical fitness can be obtained by a variety of activities, both sporting and martial art, but Kano also ensured that judo was of much more value within an educational environment.

The fact that judo is not a team game helps to develop both self esteem and a respect for others. Mutual welfare and benefit became a mantra to Kano as did such maxims as 'maximum efficiency from minimum effort'. Kano insisted that judoka learn self control and humility before they could be considered for promotion to higher grades and even to this day, the Kodokan's *dan* grading requirements are that those wishing promotion are not just proficient fighters, but indicate their understanding of the spirit of Judo and have, over a period of time, shown they have a worthy character. Such valuation would have little relevance for the gaining of qualification within a sport setting, even if what is being sought is a 'sporting attitude'.

In fact, it is questionable as to just what is meant by 'sport'. While traditional values of sport continue to be adhered to in many quarters, a modern take on professional sport is more likely to encompass a set of values that come under the heading of 'gamesmanship', whereby one is more inclined to bend the rules of a game in order to achieve victory.

As one American teacher said on discovering judo while teaching alongside Kano: "Judo is not only a means of self-defence, it incorporates elements of philosophy, economics and moral conduct."

The sporting attitude was, in actual fact, one of the key elements in the development of judo, but to say so does not equate immediately with the concept of a sport. Rather, Kano was trying to instil a set of values in his pupils that included concern for the well-being of training partners. This was essential to Kano's way of thinking, but it was also essential if he was to get judo established within an educational setting. The concept of pupils engaging in an activity that regularly resulted in injury, accidental or otherwise, would not have helped his cause. In a modern litigation society such considerations are even more relevant than they were in the founder's day.

As an interesting aside, it is of little benefit for those training in judo as a fighting system for it to be dangerous. While it is important to know the techniques that have a devastating effect, it is not practical to put them into use at each training session. To do so would result in less and less training partners, or eventually an injury to oneself that would make the exponent *hors de combat*.

Eventually judo was incorporated into the Japanese educational system in 1911. It was a major step for the development of judo, but at that stage, Kodokan judo remained a minority if high profile activity within Japan.

Outside Japan, judo was also getting a reputation as a fighting system par-excellence. This was no accident, either. Kano was keen that his art be transported around the world. Among other things, he saw it as a means of showing the western world a little of Japanese culture, but at the same time showing that Japan itself was moving away from its feudal past.

Kano's keenness to have judo spread around the world even at an early stage caused a dilution of his ideals, the ramifications of which are still with us today.

Two people who left the Kodokan to take their judo training and transplant it in other parts of the world were Mitsuyo Maeda, a 4th *dan* and Vasili Oshchepkov, a Russian 2nd *dan* product of the Kodokan.

Maeda was one of Kano's top students when he went to America as the junior partner of Tsenejiro Tomita in 1904. He quickly parted ways with Tomita, seeking instead to earn a living through challenge matches. This went against Kano's ideals.

Despite his diminutive stature Maeda proved a very adept fighter, but making a living in wrestling halls inevitably led to him adapting the techniques of judo and jettisoning some of the more esoteric rules that Kano had set out. Maeda was keen to take opponents to the ground and in halls where judo rules did not apply, was quite happy to use less orthodox methods of getting people 'into his office'.

Maeda had come through the Kodokan at the time that the Kosen's *ne-waza* techniques were holding sway and it was groundwork that he clearly preferred.

Kosen judo was geared almost solely towards groundwork. Until the change of rules in 1925 that stipulated that all moves had to start with *tachiwaza* it was acceptable to drag an opponent to the floor. From 1925 three attempts at this would lead to a disqualification in competition, but up until that point, Kosen practitioners would happily take an opponent to the ground to work on them. The almost exclusive study of *ne-waza* that they did meant that generally they were better prepared the for ground than those judoists that had been trained at either of the main judo academies, the Kodokan and the DBNK.

Eventually settling in Brazil it was Maeda that taught his style of Kosen-influenced judo to Carlos Gracie. There is continued debate about the level of realism that exists within Kodokan judo compared to that contained in what became Gracie jujutsu, or Brazilian jujutsu. The arguments are usually started on a false premise.

Gracie jujutsu was most definitely a product of judo, not jujutsu. Maeda, being removed from the still developing headquarters of judo moved in a different direction, with greater emphasis on groundwork skills, but his art, as defined by his protégés, the Gracies, continues to have a belt-ranking system and a set of contest rules. Traditional *judo gis* were also worn by practitioners, even if they later became somewhat more garish than those worn by *judoka*.

Brazilian jujutsu continues to include techniques that are banned in modern sport judo, but they are not techniques unknown to judoka.

Yet in many ways what Maeda and later the Gracies did was a step back from the developments that Kano had made. With no *kata* involved and no moral backbone to the activity as there was with Kodokan judo, Gracie jujutsu could be seen as having no merit outside the actual combat effectiveness, which by definition can be no greater than judo, since it derives almost exclusively from judo. It was this lack of depth that had caused the old jujutsu to wane in Japan before Kano revived martial activities.

Kano had incorporated techniques into judo for a variety of reasons. The core of the activity remained an effective fighting skill, but where some of the alterations were for safety reasons, others were for the need to teach principles that could be taken on, both within the dojo and in the wider world of learning: the virtues of patience and humility are aspects of judo that are as valid today as they were when first taught.

The conceptual aspect of the final defeat in judo is something that many who took up jujutsu also struggled to come to terms with. The teaching within traditional judo of an exponent staying on their feet has a double meaning: helping *uke* - the receiver - to land safely is one aspect, but another is that a person on their feet has a better chance of controlling a given situation. The point of any real-life struggle is not to tumble to the floor and hope to come out on top, it must be to keep options open and that usually involves staying on one's feet, either to depart the scene or face a new threat.

Many involved in martial arts that claim to have a greater level of realism, or those that have adapted traditional arts to what they claim is more akin to a modern street-fighting system have a misconceived conception of what is and what is not effective. The ability to disarm and dissuade an assailant from continuing a battle should suffice. The continued damage to a person beyond 'reasonable force' is usually only a sign that the attacker has a sadistic or psychotic mind. It neither proves that he or she is a good fighter, nor that they are using the most effective fighting system. As Clausewitz points out in *On War* the purpose of battle is to make the enemy withdraw.

It is these type of considerations that Kano would have taken on board when he removed *atemi* and other dangerous techniques from *randori* judo, while retaining them in the overall judo system to be studied by senior practitioners who have moved onto a greater philosophical understanding of the art.

It is also worth noting that in 1951 when Helio Gracie, the then top-most exponent of Gracie jujutsu, challenged the Kodokan system, the President of Brazil witnessed Masahiko Kimura, a former All Japan champion decisively beat the local hero despite the rules leaning in the Brazilian's favour.

In a bout that lasted 13 minutes, Gracie was repeatedly thrown, only to rise again from the softened mat. Kimura then applied an arm lock, which because of Gracie's refusal to submit resulted in a dislocated elbow. Gracie still refused to submit,

Ashigarami. Leg locks are thought by many to be the preserve of
Brazilian Jujutsu, but are part of the pantheon of judo. This
technique continues to be practiced in the *katame-no-kata,*
even though it is outlawed in *randori* and *shiai.*

suffering a head crush and bleeding ears before his family
conceded defeat.

Kimura's victory set a pattern that lasted to the end of the
century wherein each time a high-class *judoka* took to the mat
against a Gracie jujutsu opponent, despite the rules being
different from those of judo, it was the *judoka* that came off
victorious. In 1993 Hidehiko Yoshida, a world class judo exponent
from the Kodokan beat Royce Gracie in a mixed martial arts
contest. While these results are by no means a conclusive
endorsement of any shallow idea that judo is a better fighting art

than Brazilian jujutsu, it does challenge the ludicrous notion that it could possibly be the other way round.

It is widely believed that Maeda was expelled from the Kodokan for the way that he conducted himself on the continents of America and Europe, but there is no record of his expulsion, despite the fact that he is quoted as having understood that to be the case. The indication that he accepted his removal from the Kodokan shows that Maeda was fully aware that his activities, his music hall brawling and showmanship was not within the spirit of judo as defined by Kano.

Legend has it that, unlike Maeda, Oshchepkov arrived at the Kodokan with the intent of cherry picking Kano's system for a more practical combat system of his own. This is not necessarily true. Oshchepkov was only the fourth European to receive a *dan* grade direct from Kano and, in all likelihood, started to tamper with his understanding of judo long after he left the Kodokan.

On his return to Russia in 1917, Oshchepkov was invited by the then ruling Communists to help devise a practical martial art for the Soviet secret police. An attentive pupil of Kano's, he worked on producing a style of combat that was based on biomechanics. There was no mysticism to be involved in teaching judo techniques that he had learned in Japan.

From the work of Oshchepkov and others, the Russians developed *Sambo*. The new art was designed, like Kano's, to be both practical as a self-defence system, but also to carry an educational and sporting motif. Under Communist rule, *Sambo* had a number of applications and certain parts of the art were only taught to specialist military and police personnel.

On the sporting side, the Russians were keen to develop a martial art that they could call their own, but when judo was admitted in to Olympics they saw the propaganda opportunities of quickly turning their *Sambo* fighters into judo players. The changeover was not difficult for the Russians for the simple reason that *Sambo* was based largely on the technical principles of judo.

Despite the heavy influence of Oshchepkov, *Sambo* did absorb techniques from a variety of other fighting arts, both Russian and foreign. Oshchepkov would not, however, deny the Japanese influence of *Sambo* and despite the work he put in for the

Bolsheviks, he disappeared from view during the Stalinist purges of the 1930s. His disappearance typifies Stalin's methodology of getting rid of first generation revolutionaries that could dispute his rewriting of the history of the 1917 Russian Revolution.

While Sambo and Brazilian jujutsu histories can be traced directly back not just to Judo, but to the Kodokan, ironically, one of the most famous judo clubs outside of Japan, the *Budokwai*, based in London, was originally established without a judo connection.

The Budokwai was founded in 1917 by Gunji Koizumi who, like Kano, had studied *Tenshin Shinyo Ryu* jujutsu. Yet Koizumi and therefore the Budokwai had much in common with the attitudes of Doctor Kano. The London club was not established just to teach the martial ways of fighting but also the cultural aspects of what was now given the generic term of *budo*. Poetry, Buddhism, woodprints and history were all subjects that were covered within the Budokwai as well as the more obvious martial skills of *Shinyo Ryu* jujutsu and Kendo.

In fact, Kendo, like Aikido, was a martial art which very much impressed Kano. His long-term intention had been to revamp Kendo and incorporate it into judo training. While weapons' training is not an everyday part of judo, there remains some *kata* that use the *bokken* (wooden sword) and *tanto* (wooden knife) as well as the *jo* (wooden stick).

When Kano was first shown a display of Aikido, he was so impressed with the flowing, complimentary aspect of what he witnessed that he responded "This is judo".

Nevertheless, judo was gaining clear ascendance over other jutsu back in Japan and in 1920 the Budokwai resolved to write to the Kodokan and ask for a judo instructor to be sent to England. Consequently Doctor Kano made a trip to the United Kingdom that year, bringing with him one of his own fourth *dans*. During the course of his stay it became clear that the Budokwai were at one with Kano's principles. As a result the club officially became a centre for Kodokan judo, with Koizumi and the club's other resident instructor Yukio Tani being awarded second *dan* status.

Kano would have liked the Budokwai to formally become an English site of the Kodokan, but as much as the London-based

Japanese admired Kano and wished to incorporate his philosophies into their own teachings, they also wished to retain their autonomy.

Tani had had a colourful past, being a well known challenge fighter on the British music hall scene. His activities were the sort that Kano had railed against, so it would be interesting to note whether Kano was aware of this. He may, of course, have turned a blind eye to it on the basis that he felt the Budokwai important in establishing Kodokan judo in Britain. Or, of course, Tani could have renounced his past to gain acceptance within the Kodokan.

By the time that the Budokwai had re-aligned itself behind Kano, judo had ironed out most of its early technical problems. It was now established as a fighting system bound firmly by a moral code.

Free fighting was the key to development. It was through this activity that a certain moral courage could be fostered. Techniques that were approved by Kano, but not appropriate for *randori* were, as we have seen, removed and put into *kata* training, or to be taught to higher grades as stand-alones.

It was not only for safety reasons that some techniques were removed from *randori*, however. Recognising the importance of *randori*, Kano removed techniques that would spoil the basic activity of two people training in harmony. For those of later generations who took up judo merely as a combat sport, these techniques became completely irrelevant. *Katsu* (basic resuscitation techniques) eventually went the same way with the standardisation of modern first aid.

By around 1915 Kano had more or less completed his tinkering with the rules of judo. There was to be further refinements, not least the up-dating of groundwork techniques following the Kodokan's defeat against the Kosen School, but the essence of what Kano wished to teach, both technically and morally was now completed encased in the art. In 1914, the year that the First World War broke out, the Kodokan judo Magazine was launched, with the first high school championships being held that year. One year later, the curriculum of the Japanese teacher training colleges included judo within its physical education courses.

By that time Kano was a high ranking official within the Japanese education establishment. He had become Asia's first member of the Olympic Committee in 1909 and in 1911 was appointed the inaugural president of the Japan Amateur Athletics Association. He was, therefore, in an ideal position to promote judo across Japan and the world. He did so with vigour, but it is worth noting at this stage that he did not seek to put judo on a sport footing, despite the ease with which he could have done so.

While some of his former protégés were earning money around the world in music halls, challenging all-comers to fight for prize money, Kano made no effort to instigate judo as an international sport. Indeed, there are numerous quotes from the founder indicating that he did not at any stage regard his art as a sport: "Judo is the way to the most effective use of both physical and spiritual strength. By training you in attacks and defences it refines your body and your soul and helps you make the spiritual essence of judo a part of your very being. In this way you are able to perfect yourself and contribute something of value to the world. This is the final goal of judo discipline."

It could not be argued with any validity that to move from this concept to that of judo being nothing but an Olympic sport is merely progression. Kano, as we have seen, was fully alive to the Olympics and very supportive of both that movement and the idea of promoting sport as a means of physical education. Yet to him, judo remained if not outside of that philosophy, then certainly distinct within it. He said: "Although Kodokan judo begins with the *randori* and the *kata*... it is based on the principles of physical education and lays stress on the harmonious development of body muscles. The principle described as the way to use body and mind most efficiently is indeed the great principle of humanity. It is a moral doctrine."

We can see clearly that Kano had an over-arching view of education and sport within that setting, but equally clearly he regarded judo as something more than a sport that had an educational benefit. Whilst many sports can claim to have a moral aspect, none, by definition, can claim that it *is* a moral doctrine.

To move from this position to regarding judo as solely a sport is not a progression, as such, but rather a deliberate diversion from the aims established by the founder.

3. Wazari
The Japanese method travels the world

The period between the two World Wars is seen by many as the golden years of judo. Membership of the Kodokan stood at over 36,000 by 1926, rising to 79,000 by 1936. Kano himself was travelling extensively around the world, partly to promote judo, but mainly as a representative of either the Japanese government or the International Olympic Committee.

He was keen that judo was transmitted across the globe, so not only did he take every opportunity to promote it himself, he also picked emissaries to take his teachings and ideals to places that he could not visit himself.

He was aware that some of those that took judo across the seas had resorted to music hall activities to pay their way. This he was not keen on. To the founder it was vitally important that his art be taken seriously as a moral teaching. It was, therefore as important not to get trapped into any musical hall activity as it was to avoid the bad old ways of jujutsu.

Perhaps it was fortunate for Kano that in many places during this period there was little or no understanding of the difference between judo and jujutsu. In Japan this was not the case, but elsewhere judo was often presented as jujutsu, or 'The Japanese Method'. Under such guises, judo was rapidly becoming the unarmed combat of choice for the world's military and police bodies.

During this period, and even after the Second World War, judo manuals gave clear indications of judo as a method of self-defence. Wrist locks, shoulder locks and *ataemi*, striking arts, were all illustrated with instruction as to how and when they could best be used in self-defence.

The Japanese authorities themselves were happy to have judo as a means of training their military and police organisations. Kano certainly collaborated in this; he had pitched judo against other jutsu from the beginning and had also colluded with the establishment of the Butokukai, which glorified the old samurai mentality.

Yet he was known to have drawn a line that he did not want crossed. The Emperor was keen for the Kodokan to be turned into a military establishment for the training of his troops at a time when Japanese imperialism was growing. Kano would not approve this. To do so would have relegated judo to a mere combat activity, so he resisted the overtures. Instead he continued to ensure that all the high grades that left the Kodokan on teaching missions fully understood the wider implications of his art.

Kano therefore kept a close eye on how judo was perceived. Where he could, when he sent high-graded *judoka* out as emissaries, he funded them to ensure that they did not resort to the sort of activities that had caused Maeda to devise his own fighting system. The aim was still to promote the spirit as much as the techniques of judo.

To that end, gradings within the Kodokan were important and indeed remain so. High graded Kodokan *judoka* only acquired their grades once Kano was satisfied as to the character of the individual concerned. This attitude is reflected in the dan grade requirements of the Kodokan to this day. The current guidelines from the Kodokan state: "In screening candidates for dan promotion, personality, acquirement of judo spirit, extent of the understanding of judo and mastery of technical arts, practical application of judo in everyday life, and contribution to judo are considered. Those who are mean in character and whose speech and behaviour are deviated from judo spirit will not be promoted irrespective of any other merit."

This is a very clear indication that judo is not, even in its current form, just a combat sport; certainly not as far as the Kodokan is concerned. Indeed the world centre of judo continues to accept the precept that to be considered a good *judoka*, i.e., to gain a senior grade, fighting prowess is only one of the criteria set down.

Kano, then, in the inter-war period was careful to ensure that the people he sent around the world to promote judo fully understood the implications of their grades.

It was in the early 1930s that the All Japan Championships were inaugurated. This contest remains today as one of the most significant in the Japanese judo calendar. There are no weight categories and originally the scoring did not include the lower scores of *koka* (three points) or *yuko* (five points). Wins were on the basis of two *ippons* (10 points each) or an accumulation of *wazaris* (seven points each). The lower scores, introduced in the 1960s, simply did not fit the attacking spirit of judo.

The establishment of the All Japan Championships, which followed on from the Emperor's Cup as the foremost judo contest was not a signal that Kano had altered his attitude to judo as a contest sport. He had constantly suggested that competition was a valid way of proving one's spiritual and physical development: it was a useful means to an end, not the summit of one's activity.

In 1931 Kano wrote: "Judo is a mental and physical discipline whose lessons are readily applicable to our daily affairs. The fundamental principle of judo is that whatever the objective, it is best attained by the maximum efficient use of mind and body for that purpose. The same principle applied to our everyday activities leads to the highest and most rational life.

"Training in judo is not the only way to grasp this, but it is how I arrived at an understanding of it, and it is the means I attempt to enlighten others.

"The principle demands above all that there be order and harmony among people. The final aim of judo is to inculcate respect for the principles of maximum efficiency and respect for the principles of maximum efficiency and mutual welfare and benefit. Through judo, persons individually and collectively attain their highest spiritual state while at the same time developing their bodies and learning the art of attack and defence."

In this definition of the activity which he created, Kano did not once mention the word 'sport.'

It is perhaps a concept which many who get involved in martial arts and all those who become involved in sport have trouble adapting to. Kano himself entered the world of martial arts for the express purpose of learning an effective self-defence system. As he travelled his personal road, the aims of his training changed. It is an experience met many times over by those that followed his path. Conceptually, the idea of improving oneself both physically and mentally is one that comes with diligent training. The repetitive act of *uchikomi* can be seen by outsiders as merely the training required to make a technique work. Rarely, however, will anybody become tuned into the greater meaning of judo or any other martial art without that same *uchikomi* practice taking on a greater significance. The in-depth study becomes a means of enlightenment, a means of looking both at the art of what one is trying to achieve and the person, i.e., self, that is trying to achieve the best results they can. The study for harmonisation with one's training partner becomes a desire to be at one within. From this feeling of strength it is possible to move on technically and emotionally.

These ideas may seem mystic to western people and as Japan becomes more and more westernised, some Japanese too will fail to grasp them. However, those that remain at the forefront of Kodokan judo take these lessons on board. For those values to be retained in a world of mixed martial arts and Olympic judo it is important that a significant number of coaches at all levels foster a broader attitude to judo than that which currently prevails in organisations that concentrate on money and a medal count.

With its grappling aspect and the need to train with another, judo has a greater opportunity to promote this than the striking arts, while other grappling arts have sprung up with little or no ethical aspect to their core values.

The writing of later generations of world-renowned *judoka*, such as Katsuhiko Kashiwazaki, indicates that the ideals of Kano have not been totally lost.

Kashiwazaki was an All-Japan weight category champion on five occasions and a world champion in 1981. Recognised as one of the best fighting *judoka* of his generation, he too spoke of the spiritual aspects of Judo: "The *budo* attach great importance to refining the spirit in addition to forging the body through technique. The Kodokan's three purposes are physical education, contest and virtuous spirit.

"Through ascetic training in judo one can refine the virtues and intellect and the principles of contest can be applied to every aspect of human life."

Kashiwazaki would appreciate the difference between winning a point by fluke and performing a perfect technique. In sport, the point, as delivered by the referee, is the be-all and end-all. Yet when practicing judo as a *budo*, rather than as a sport, an individual will understand the importance of achieving the ends by the correct method.

Further evidence of Kano's disinterest in turning judo into a pure and simple sport can clearly be seen by the number of other activities within Kodokan judo that were considered as integral to Judo training at this time: *kata* remained of importance, not just the *randori-no-kata*, those that promoted good *randori* practice, but others, too. The *itsutsu-no-kata*, even by the founder's recognition bore no relevance at all to sport judo. There was little benefit to the sport judo player studying *katsu*, resuscitation methods, or how to handle a number of weapons. Yet these remained core activities for *judoka* throughout Kano's lifetime.

Even before his death, however, Kano had to deal with exponents of judo that had not fully understood what he wanted judo to represent. At one point, in order to enlighten those that were over-emphasising the sporting aspect of judo he said: "If you want to know what I truly intended for judo, then look at what they are doing at the Kodokan women's section."

Kano had taken women on as his students at a very early stage of Kodokan judo. There had been some raised eyebrows on this from more traditional Japanese minds, but in a typical response to their concerns, Kano seriously looked at the claims that judo could be (more) damaging to the health of females than males. Inevitably, after extensive research, he decided that judo was just as beneficial to females as to males.

What was clear, however, was that usually women were not as interested in the competitive side of judo. At the time this would have been just as well. Despite his inclination to include women in judo activity, the concept of joint training would not have gone down well in wider Japanese society. As it was, Kano involved his entire family in judo. His first female student was enrolled in 1893 and Kano also taught both his wife and daughters judo. The Kodokan opened its first official women's section in 1925 and for a number of years the head of that section was Kano's eldest daughter, Noriko Watanuki.

The *ju-no-kata*, the *kata* of suppleness, was devised with the idea that it would demonstrate the self-defence aspects of judo as well as being an exercise that was useful in terms of physical education. The author can vouch for the latter by virtue of the fact that once he started training regularly at the *ju-no-kata*, a niggling back pain that he had suffered for some years was considerably eased.

A greater understanding of the *ju-no-kata* also leads towards a greater understanding of the basic ideas of balance-breaking, one of the key factors in helping Kodokan judo gain ascendancy over other jutsu in the first place.

One of Kano's earliest female students was Keiko Fukuda, who was the daughter of one of Kano's original jujutsu instructors. Fukuda went on to attain the grade of 9th dan and is the last living link with Kano. She was clear that contest was not the essence of judo passed down to her from the founder. Fukuda became the first - and currently only - female to attain a Kodokan 9th dan. She now lives and coaches in the USA.

Other *kata* that *judoka* were and still are supposed to study include a specific self-defence *kata*, a *kata* of 'ancient forms' which represent battlefield manoeuvres conducted in full samurai armour and a *kata* which merely demonstrates, according to Kano, the 'heart of judo'. Currently, self-defence techniques are understood through the *Goshin-jutsu kata*, devised by the Kodokan in 1956. In recognition of modern times the kata involves defence against kicks, punches and grabs as well as knife, stick and gun threats.

These are strange activities indeed for a sport. The truth is, of course, that during this 'golden period' of judo, the activity was not considered by Kano or his followers to be a sport in any real sense. A sporting element there was, but a sport, it was not.

In 1935 the Kodokan introduced the *Seiryoku Zen'Yo Kokumin Taiku no kata* to the women's section. This *kata* demonstrated the principles of maximum efficiency and emphasised striking methods of self-defence.

Kano had from the very beginning recognised the validity of striking methods (*atemi*) within judo, the self-defence system. Yet he had not found a way of incorporating *atemi waza* into *randori*. For him *randori* remained the central activity for *judoka*. *Randori* is the way that people put together techniques in a fast-moving environment. Against a training partner who is as eager to win the contest, adding *atemi-waza* to the grappling arts would simply make the activity too dangerous and scrappy. As a training

32

method it would be reduced on several levels with such an addition.

To say that it would be dangerous is not to suggest that judo is a neutered fighting skill; far from it. *Randori* is the key element to training the mind as much as the body for a self-defence situation. Punching and kicking are undoubtedly effective fighting methods, but to use them for regular training with another person is not always practical.

Equally Kano recognised the efficacy of locks beyond the elbow lock allowed in contest judo. Such techniques along with the attack on pressure points are all part of the pantheon of judo as envisaged and devised by the founder.

Elbow locks are retained in contest judo on the basis that they are in fact the safest locks to administer in a situation whereby *uki*, the receiver, is slow in admitting defeat. Other joints receive greater damage at a lower pain threshold.

It is interesting then, to note that books written by judo experts from the 1930s nearly all contain sections on judo that do not apply to the contest and sport aspect of the art. One such legendary work was penned by Kyuzo Mifune.

Mifune had started his judo training in 1903. He arrived in Tokyo with a burning desire to be part of the Kodokan at a time when personal recommendation was the way through the door. Knowing no-one inside the establishment, Mifune harassed a senior member to get his required recommendation and did not look back.

Fifteen months after signing his blood-oath to the Kodokan, Mifune was a first *dan*, four months later he was a second *dan*. It was a remarkable rise for a remarkable man. Mifune went on to be promoted 6th *dan* by 1912. Reputedly never beaten in contest he was an annual winner of the Red and White contests at the Kodokan and in 1937 Kano promoted him to 9th *dan*. He received his 10th *dan* in 1945.

On Kano's death Mifune became the inspiration and leader of Kodokan judo. He was known simply as the 'God of judo' and was revered almost as much as the founder himself. In his book *The Canon of Judo*, Mifune wrote: "Judo is the acquisition of moral and physical discipline and martial arts training." In defining martial arts he said this meant: "to reasonably defend oneself."

Like Kano, Mifune knew full well that judo was a synthesis. It remained essentially a fighting art par excellence, but one with an integral sporting element, which was equally important in terms of its promotion within an educational setting. It also contained at its kernel a philosophy that is contradictory to both positions. Mifune wrote: "In judo competition, one's approach should be resolute, as if you exist between life and death, but this should not entail any kind of violence. 'To exist between life and death' does not mean simply to live and to die. The attitude the student must seek is a vow to embody reality, without purposefully 'seeking death' or 'devaluing one's own life', as these are anachronistic and romantic military notions."

The Canon of Judo is essentially a technical manual for contest judo, yet despite this and Mifune's own success in this area, he makes his philosophical understanding of judo clear: "Judo is based on a virtuous philosophy, separating right from wrong. It is considerably more than just a fighting art. It is a passage from 'jutsu' to 'do' – this is judo's enlightenment."

Mifune's words were echoed by Kenji Tomiki, another of the inter-war greats to emerge from the Kodokan. Tomiki was a Kodokan 8th *dan*, who went on to gain the same grade in Aikido. Like Mifune, Tomiki was on the Kodokan's technical committee. Tomiki too was keen to state that judo had a philosophical aspect that distanced it from jujutsu. He said simply: "A martial art that has no rules is nothing but violence," before stating clearly that the free practice of *randori* was of more significance than *shiai*. "*Randori* practise is something that is done to give life to the real power of those techniques that were learned through *kata*. That is to say, *randori* provides the power to complete a painted dragon by filling in the eyes."

Yet judo was, even in his own lifetime starting to run away from Kano. He clearly wished to see it spread around the world, but as more and more people became involved inevitably others wished to take the activity in different directions. While the Emperor of Japan had plans of turning the Kodokan into a quasi-military establishment, at the other end of the scale the sport aspect was becoming equally as popular.

There were moves to have judo turned into an Olympic sport even in Kano's time and with the Olympics scheduled to take place in Japan in 1940 that seemed a likely opportunity to promote such an inclusion. Yet Kano himself, despite his heavy involvement with the Olympic movement, was not keen. Having spent many years insisting that judo was more than a sport, the nearest he got to endorsing judo's inclusion in the Olympics was in a 1936 conversation with Koizumi, when he said: "I have been asked by people of various sections as to the wisdom and possibility of judo being introduced with other games and sports at the Olympic Games. My view on the matter, at present, is rather passive. If it be the desire of other member countries I have no objection. But I do not feel inclined to take any initiative. For one thing, judo, in reality, is not a mere sport or game. I regard it as a principle of life, art and science. In fact it is a means for personal cultural attainment. Only one of the forms of judo training, so-called *randori* or free practice, can be classed as a form of sport. Certainly, to some extent, the same may be said of boxing and fencing, but today they are practised and conducted as sports. Then, the Olympic Games are so strongly flavoured with nationalism that it is possible to be influenced by it and to develop 'contest judo', a retrograde form as jujutsu was before Kodokan judo was founded."

It is a telling passage. Kano foresaw the rise of contest judo and recognised that if it were over-emphasised it would negate the hard work that he had put into developing a cultural and spiritual aspect to judo.

He was clearly disappointed with the way that some contest-oriented people took judo even in his own life time. After watching one particular bout he said to those competing: "You fought like young bulls locking horns; there was nothing about any of the techniques I witnessed today. I never taught anyone to do Kodokan judo like that. If all you think about is winning through brute strength, that will be the end of Kodokan judo."

It was not to be however. The switch of emphasis that Kano had noted was already gathering momentum. During the 1920s and 1930s there were many who did not share Kano's attitude. Sport and the Olympics had become a political and economic powerhouse. There was, as there is now, intense rivalry between nations to host the event and within that rivalry there were various agendas being promoted.

Kano's ideals may have matched those of Pierre de Coubertin, the founder of the modern Olympics, but like Coubertin's event, judo was beginning to outgrow and move away from the ideals set down by its founder.

Following the first international match between England's Budokwai and clubs based in Germany in 1929, the Germans had been keen to develop judo as an international sporting medium. Unlike Kano they were happy to consider judo as merely a sport and equally important they fully understood the politicisation of sport. Alongside the training of the Hitler Youth Movement in judo during the 1930s, the Germans campaigned for the inclusion of judo in the 1940s Olympics. Those Olympics did not take place because of the outbreak of the Second World War.

Kano himself died, some suggest mysteriously, in 1938 on board a homebound ship after another of his epic fact-finding trips to the other side of the world. He had been an outspoken critic of Japan's militarization and viewed the Olympics as a means of bringing about world harmony. He had, on that basis, worked tirelessly on behalf of the Olympic committee.

Just weeks after his death, Japan pulled the plug on the 1940 Games, another inexorable step towards world conflagration.

With the event of an All Japan Championship and the spread of judo across the world it was inevitable that tensions would exist between various factions as to the true merits of judo. Kano himself had started training with the concept of jutsu being nothing more than a self-defence system. He modified techniques on the basis of their efficacy, but as time progressed he also started to view the activity as something more than a mere fighting skill. "Crucially I did not stress only training for fighting," he said.

The practicality of Kodokan judo as a fighting art was not to be abandoned, however. The training methods continued to ensure that judo was the art of choice for organisations such as the Tokyo Police and as we have seen the Kodokan was coveted by the Japanese imperial military machine. Kano had got judo onto the national school curriculum on the basis of the educational values of the art and of course, there continued to be the aspect of Judo as a means of self-fulfilment and development, a less tangible, but nevertheless very valuable part

36

of Kano's vision. Additionally with the advent of contests and competitions, both internally within Japan and internationally, for example between British and German clubs, the idea of judo as a sport was starting to take hold.

In Europe there were moves to establish a European Judo Union, the espoused idea being to standardise the rules. With Kano still alive and the Kodokan still producing instructors, that seems a spurious desire. Kano was certainly keen on the establishment of a worldwide organisation, but one can be sure that the Kodokan, which had a technical committee, was more than capable of establishing the rules for its own activity.

The rules of judo competition had been more-or-less established in 1900, when Kano worked through the differences between the Kodokan and the Butokukai. Part of the problem was the on-going dispute as to just how much time should be spent in *newaza*. In collusion with the Butokukai, Kano allowed, perhaps against his better judgement, a person to use drag-down methods to get an opponent into ground work if that was their area of expertise. As he explained: "When we were formulating that rule, we felt there would be few negative effects but when we implemented it we discovered it was flawed. We decided to revise the rule and after many meetings we formulated the revised judging in 1922." Revisions continued for another three years.

In any case, the outbreak of the Second World War stopped the idea of a European Union. Judo had established itself very strongly in both Britain and Germany with a number of joint summer schools being set up, but with the two nations taking opposite positions in the fight against fascism, the *judoka* of each country found the opportunities of working together removed.

It is interesting to note, at this point, that the fascist countries of Germany and Italy both objected to women being involved in judo. The leadership in both countries believed that women should not be involved in such activities, instead, preferring the view of the Roman Catholic Church and suggesting that women should concentrate on their roles as wives and mothers.

Put into a historical perspective, women were not regarded as equal citizens anywhere else in the world either, but they were certainly not barred from taking up judo in Britain as they were in the fascist countries.

In fact, women had usually been involved in judo at the Budokwai almost since its inception. The first female member of the club was Katherine White-Cooper, who was registered in April 1919 as member number 60. Mixed classes, however, were not the norm, but the club did have a very successful series of women-only classes, the emphasis not being on *randori*, but on *kata* and self-defence. Often the teacher at these sessions was Koizumi himself. It is not difficult to understand why the self-defence aspect of judo was appealing. The basic tenant that a physically smaller person can overcome a more powerfully built assailant is perfectly tuned for women concerned for their safety in a boisterous male-dominated society.

By the time the World War impacted fully on Japan in 1941, Kano had been dead for three years. His nephew, Jiro Kano took over the running of the organisation at a time when there was huge pressure from the Emperor to ensure that the Kodokan and the Butokukai were fully utilised as a place where military techniques could be taught. Although the two organisations were close and the Kodokan continued to provide top level instructors for the Butokukai, there were distinct differences, not only in style, but in their attitude to the government. Whilst Kano, the head of the Kodokan, was a patriot with no sense of imperialism, the Butokukai was run by a very different establishment, one that was steeped in Japanese imperialism and funded by the government. It was not in a position to resist the moves to militarization.

4. Ippon
Olympics, Olympians and martial artists

The Second World War and its aftermath wrought heavy changes on judo. Kano had already been dead for some three years before Japan entered the Pacific conflict, but in any case there were external pressures being brought to the way judo was being perceived and therefore performed.

Japan entered the conflict in December 1941 and by March 1942 the Butokukai was made subordinate to the Japanese war effort, instructing in martial skills relevant to the military. The Kodokan had little choice in the matter and followed suit in September of the same year, falling under the administrative control of the Butokukai, an irony no doubt noted by senior Kodokan members. Judo as sport was deemed an irrelevance. Contest was shelved as the straightforward hand-to-hand combat aspect of judo was promoted.

After the completion of the American occupation of Japan in 1945, the Americans were naturally keen to shut off Japan's military establishments. They were keen also, to track down Japan's hard-line fascist activists and in October 1945 the Supreme Commander Allied Powers, General MacArthur, decreed that "Dissemination of militaristic and ultra-nationalistic ideology will be prohibited and all military education and drill will be discontinued." The Butokukai was closed.

The myth is that judo was then made illegal in Japan, but in fact it occupied a rather grey area. Many of the instructors connected with the Butokukai were those that the Americans wished to remove from the arena of public life and certainly judo was banned from schools and other public institutions except for the police.

Yet the ban was only partial and over a period of time the activity gradually regained its popularity through private clubs. The Kodokan itself was allowed to reopen once it had satisfied the occupying powers that it had reverted to its former position and renounced the militaristic ethos that the Imperial powers had imposed on it.

There were, of course, many high quality *judoka* still around after the end of hostilities. A key figure was Kyuzo Mifune, who had been a direct disciple of Kano. Mifune's emphasis on the purity of judo helped the rehabilitation of the Kodokan. The Butokukai was a different proposition, however. It had always been closer to the Imperial state than the Kodokan. It had always had a different remit to the Kodokan and its leading lights were mostly considered to be inoculated with Japanese imperialism.

With the Butokukai taken out of the equation the popularisation of judo across the world from the late 1940s on was down to a number of high-class individuals who travelled the world in a way that would have made Kano proud: Kenshiro Abbe, an 7th *dan* from the Butokukai, arrived in Britain in 1955, his *kata* partner Hachi Mitchigami pitched up in France and Ichiro Abe did work in Belgium. Abbe and Mitchigami, along with the likes of Kimura, were proud of their attachment to the Butokukai, but under the new regime they were forced to realign themselves to the Kodokan.

At the time of writing, Abe is one of just three living Kodokan 10th *dan*. Yet by the time these wonderful *judoka* had set sail, even in Japan judo was undergoing a massive change due to the outcome of the Second World War and the American occupation.

American servicemen were particularly keen on judo as a genuine example of Japanese culture – a robust physical activity that young fighting men were, and still are, likely to appreciate. In fact American judo history is heavily influenced by the Second World War experience of their servicemen.

Yoshitsugu Yamishita had been one of Kano's early emissaries to the USA, arriving in 1904 and teaching President Theodore Roosevelt some judo, but it was not until after the Second World War that America really took to the activity when young men returned from the conflict with the judo knowledge they had gained in Japan.

Even so there was no real attempt to bring it all together until the 1950s. During that decade judo was added to the curriculum of the US Air Command and the American Forces Judo Association was established. In 1952 a delegation that contained Sumiyuki Kotani, later 10th *dan* and Kenji Tomiki, the founder of *Tomiki Aikido* and the man who developed the Kodokan's *Goshin jutsu kata*, arrived in America to train a team. This delegation is recognised as being the major influence on the fledgling American judo scene.

While the authorities were slow in allowing judo back into Japanese schools, the activity continued to develop outside official channels, eventually bringing pressure to bear for its return to the school syllabus.

It was clear, however, that a complete return to pre-war days was not possible. The All Japan Judo League was established in 1948 and worked hard to have judo re-established in schools. In rejecting the pleas, the American establishment continually made reference to the use that the military authorities had made of judo during the war. To combat that propaganda, judo enthusiasts had to flag up the educational benefits of their activity – there was plenty of writing from the founder to back them up. In a 1949 appeal to the Ministry of Education the League pointed out that judo was acceptable in the country at large and should be as well for schools: "The *budo* sports were misused by militaristic and ultra-nationalistic people during the war. It does not mean they are militaristic," they claimed indignantly.

While such appeals were being launched many Japanese people were returning to judo. Authorities were tipped off regarding a *dojo* that had been established in a basement at Chuo University and on investigation they found a *dojo* complete with *judogi* hanging from the walls ready for practice. When challenged, the University admitted that the basement had indeed been set aside for judo practice, but the University was not responsible for any breaking of the law since it did not subsidise the activity and it did not provide the tuition.

Evidence of the growth of judo immediately after the war is cited by the Kodokan's membership, which rose to 225,497 by 1946. A year earlier Mifune had been promoted to 10th *dan*.

Mifune was regarded by many as being the 'God of judo'. A small man in stature, he was in a position of great authority after the war in terms of the technical direction that judo took. In the foreword of his book *The Canon of Judo,* written in 1954, he spoke of judo taking on a "new meaning and significance".

It had become clear that to facilitate judo's complete reintegration into mainstream Japanese post-war culture the accent had to be on judo as a sport. Time and again the Japan Judo League petitioned the government to have judo reintroduced into the national school curriculum. Each time they pointed out the benefits of judo in terms of physical development, often attaching the idea that spiritual progress could also be made for individual participants. Close combat skills were kept out of the equation, despite the fact that it was quietly acknowledged that senior members of the Kodokan were still schooled in *atemi-waza* and other fighting skills not relevant to contest judo. Judo, in the mainstream, had to be neutered of its street-fighting aspects and promoted as a combat sport with a spiritual element.

This was not necessarily a bad thing, even from a traditionalist perspective. Kano himself had moved on from the days that he learned *jujutsu* merely as a self-defence system. Kodokan judo had moved with its founder until his death. However, Kano had been keen to ensure that the sport element of judo did not overshadow all other aspects. Certainly he was happy that judo should be used as a form of personal development, which allowed the mind and body to develop together.

However, the emphasis placed on sport judo led inexorably to judo becoming an Olympic sport with all the modern attitudes that incorporates.

The forward march to Olympic sport status continued to be headed up outside Japan. Following the ending of the Second World War, Europeans again returned to the idea of a European Judo Union, one that would ensure that the rules of the 'game' were able to facilitate cross-border competition.

If Kano himself would have baulked at such a move, one of Europe's leading *judoka* certainly realised that the genie was being released from the bottle.

Kenji Koizumi had spoken to Kano before the latter's death about the establishment of a European judo organisation and Koizumi was once again at the forefront as *judoka* from half-a-dozen countries gathered to form the European Judo Federation in 1948.

There were now a series of rapid developments that pushed the sporting aspect of judo to the front in a way that had never happened before. While the Japanese judo organisations were struggling to gain acceptance of their activity as a sport, the Europeans were pushing on with their federal ideas. The British Judo Association was formed in 1948. Three years later the International Judo Federation was formed.

Chairing the meeting that established the EJU was Trevor Leggett, a veteran of the Kodokan whose later writings show clearly that he was imbibed with, and understood, the full holistic aspects of judo. Yet from the chair Leggett spelt out the purpose of establishing an international body. The proposal, he said, was "the standardisation of judo rules and the establishment of an international body for arbitration". It was an echo of pre-war ideas that Europeans could head up the standardisation of what was essentially a Japanese invention and once again ignored the fact that the Kodokan was quite capable of establishing its own modus operandi and indeed had been doing so since its inception. The irony of this imperialistic attitude was almost certainly lost on the self-aggrandising westerners.

Judo as sport was now overshadowing every other aspect of the activity as competitions were being promoted across the board. In 1951 the EJF re-jigged itself to become the International Judo Federation, setting up a new European Judo Union in its wake. Progress, if that is what these new, sporting developments were, was rapid, but not everybody, even in the west, was comfortable as they realised that judo was moving away from a multi-faceted activity to a one-dimensional function.

In his message to the IJF in 1952, Aldo Torti, the EJU president, highlighted the problem that was already starting to tug at the heart of judo: "I asked Risei Kano if, following Japanese precepts, judo had to be considered primarily as a sport, or as something else. I was answered that, according to Kano's last writings, judo was *also* [my italic] a sport. This question is of importance because it is only if judo is just a sport, and nothing else, that it is then possible to speak of a federation." Torti ignored his own logic and continued that the EJU should present the sport of judo to the world.

Koizumi, who was unequivocally the leading exponent of judo in Europe and had indeed been the driving force behind the wider concept of federalisation, was beginning to realise where the post-war developments were leading. He made his discomfort clear in the same year that the EJU came into being. He told the meeting: "When I was coming along this morning I was sorry, not only for myself but for all of you, that I was the instrument of your not being able to enjoy this lovely country and lovely weather today. From the way you have been struggling to solve the pressing problems at this conference, it seems that you are suffering from a sort of toothache which you do not know how to cure! That means that all these problems arose from the basis of competition - championships and international contests. For a cure, I should like to advise you to extract this tooth - that is, to do away altogether with championships and international competition.

"To appreciate judo, its benefits and value, you must actually taste and enjoy it. That means you must partake of judo training. Like food, unless you eat and enjoy the flavour and the quality of the food, you cannot appreciate its goodness. So it was on Friday, after two or three hours' hard struggle discussing the technical problems of this conference, we were invited to go to Mr Graf's *dojo*, and there on the mat we all mixed - seven nations - practising judo and partaking of training together. You ought to have seen the effect of that completely changed atmosphere, and the feeling of the people! There was no question of weight categories or other problems.

"We enjoyed the beer afterwards and the taste of the food, which completely changed after those two hours' training on the mat. That is judo. Without that there is no judo. You cannot express the realities of life. However wise or clever, they are always insufficient in terms of human language. Any move you may bring forward, if it is not to produce the result that judo aims at, you are defeating its own end. Therefore, you must be very careful what you do today. Good positive work has been accomplished here, that is absolutely certain. Please do not make rules that are too hard and too fast. That is all I have to say. Thank you."

Clearly there was a schism opening up in the world of judo. The people that wished to promote judo as a combat sport had the upper hand. In Japan itself, the concept of judo as sport had to be promoted to return judo to be a mainstream activity, something that it finally achieved when judo was once again taught in schools from 1950 onwards. In Europe, 1951 saw the first organised European Championships.

It was not until the following year that Japan joined the IJF. When they did so the presidency was immediately given to Risei Kano. To those not following the historical developments, it could now appear that judo was merely picking up where the outbreak of the Second World War had left it, with the son of the founder taking his place at the head of what was now a world organisation. Judo was not only becoming big, however, it was becoming commercial and it was becoming a sport.

Olympic recognition was something that many had hankered for since even before the death of Kano. With a World Championship established in 1956 and the Games heading for Tokyo in 1964, the opportunity to place judo squarely in the frame was quickly looming. All efforts of the international organisation were geared towards that end.

The EJU and the IJF had been set up specifically to look at rules of contest to enable competition across the globe. They quickly realised that if judo was to make it to Olympic qualification then a number of changes needed to be made.

To that point, rule changes had been about how to maximise training opportunities, safety factors and ensuring that the activity was free-flowing. The 1925 rule change has seen the elbow finally became the only joint that was to be locked. Finger locks, toe, wrist and ankle locks had all been allowed in judo up to 1899 and, right up until the 1950s, there was still no time limit on a contest. Now rules had to be altered to take into account the Olympics.

In the past contests had gone on until one or other combatant was exhausted, or the referee decided enough was enough. This simply could not continue if judo was to take its place on the Olympic stage. Originally a 20-minute limit was imposed on a contest, but over the years this was reduced until the current time whereby *dan*-grade competition is down to just five minutes; many *kyu*-grade contests being bouts of just three minutes.

One of the most controversial changes of the post-war period, however, was the introduction of weight categories. The first World Championships, held in Tokyo in 1956 had not had weight-categories, instead grade being seen as the more relevant

45

division. This was also the case in 1961 in Paris. At that time, the Europeans were keen on weight categories, the Japanese were not. What happened at those championships, however, changed the perspectives of even the tradition-minded Japanese.

The winning of the title of World Champion, by Dutchman Anton Geesink threw the judo world into turmoil. Geesink was a 127kg (20 stone), 1.98 metres (6 feet 6 inches) man-mountain and his victory against the Japanese Koji Sone shook the Japanese. To have a single champion of their sport that was not Japanese was almost unthinkable. The day after Geesink's triumph the Japanese accepted the argument regarding categories and the IJF introduced four weight categories.

Traditionalists were up in arms. Using weight categories, they argued, took away the concept that a small man or woman should be able to throw a larger opponent. In self-defence terms this is, of course, an accepted concept, but in sport terms it had no relevance. A contest must be seen to be even for a modern spectator sport and weight categories were essential in this. Significantly, grading events continued to run without weight categories, but the shift towards sport was inexorable and weight categories were an essential way of opening the sport up.

Geesink may have been, by Japanese standards, a monster of a man, but he clearly aligned himself with a traditional, Japanese, approach to judo. On winning the world title he travelled to Japan to continue his studies and his earnest approach to judo gained him respect in the land of judo's origin, even if his victory against Sone had caused embarrassment and soul searching.

Yet Geesink had not finished with Japanese sensibilities. Three years after his world title success he was to shake the Japanese to the core at the 1964 Olympics when he won the heavyweight title, again defeating a Japanese opponent in the process.

The Japanese took three of the four golds on offer in 1964. It took Geesink eight minutes to overcome Kaminaga. In doing so, however, he opened up judo to a much wider, western audience. For the Japanese it was a bitter pill to swallow, but in the long term Geesink had, for the second time done judo a huge favour. Having been instrumental in getting weight categories instituted he now showed clearly that the rest of the world were more than capable of competing against the Japanese: his victory in Paris could not now be put down to any sort of freak.

Despite the damage that he did to their self-esteem, the Japanese took Geesink to their heart. It is not difficult to understand why. The Dutchman credited his Japanese coaches for his victory and was quick to absorb the wider lessons of judo.

While many traditionalists complained of the introduction of weight categories, there were some clear benefits to be had. It is true that many top class *judoka* from across the generations have been physically small people who have trained hard to make their techniques work on larger people. However, there are an untold number of people that have failed to make their way even into the *dojo* as the thought of taking on physically large people has turned them against the idea of judo. The old maxim that 'a good big one will always beat a good little one', too, had ensured that when it comes to a contest, smaller people are at a clear disadvantage.

Once judo had moved into the realms of a spectator sport a number of changes were inevitable. Certainly, the changes did not occur all at once, but in hindsight many were unavoidable if judo was to take up the opportunity of massive expansion.

Fighting on the ground had been an important part of judo since Kano's Kodokan people learned their lesson the hard way against those from the Kosen school, but progressively ground fighting had more and more limitations imposed on it because it was difficult, from a referee's and a spectator's point of view, to see exactly what was happening. Groundwork, therefore, had to be clear.

Not allowing competitors more time to develop a move on the ground was, like the introduction of weight categories, another change that irritated traditionalists. As Kano was aware some fighters were more naturally inclined to be good in groundwork and decreasing the time they had to develop a winning strategy in any contest was moving the activity away from certain people.

It was a far greater problem than the introduction of weight categories. As clubs geared themselves to teach a style of judo that was universal and fitted into internationally recognised rules inevitably groundwork suffered. The benefit of such a dramatic change is hard to see beyond the fact that it makes for easier viewing if contests are conducted with the contestants largely on their feet.

The tactics required for a bout were changing as the emphasis of judo activity switched from *randori* to *shiai*.

Mat craft, the use of small tactics to offset an opponent's supposed or potential superiority in skill, has probably been in existence from judo's very beginning. The art is in itself based on 'tricks', which help surprise and overcome an opponent. It is natural, therefore, that exponents will be readily inclined to seek out the boundaries of what they can do to off balance their opponent, both metaphorically and physically.

Such tactical consideration became increasingly significant as judo moved ever-closer to creating a world-wide, professional elite.

The introduction in 1974 of the minor scores of *koka* (three points) and *yuko* (five points) gave a rapid impetus to this trend. It was a change that had a far greater effect on how judo was practiced than any other post-war alteration to the rules.

Tactically, this was a boon to many sport *judoka*. It meant that they could attempt to rack up a number of potentially bout-winning scores without ever attempting to score with a direct, full-on attack. Such attacks are integral to a traditionalist's perspective because they are seen as character building: the fear of defeat, of being thrown by a counter must be controlled in the effort to find perfection in the technique. Boldness of action begets boldness of the spirit and every teacher of traditional judo is wary of teaching counters and sacrifice techniques too early in a pupil's career for fear of the students becoming inhibited fighters. Certainly they reject the ideas of teaching their pupils how to win by simply playing for low scores.

Yet it was soon learnt by those that saw judo as nothing but a combat sport that an early *koka* score, well defended thereafter, could add up to a very successful result. Time wasting was suddenly a major tactical ploy that could be used in medal winning bouts.

The knock-on effect was serious. Despite the fact that many clubs did not possess anybody with championship aspirations, *koka* training became a norm. Players who would once have had occasional coaching in how to use judo techniques without a jacket, the better to understand its self-defence application, were now being taught how to gain a minor score. Grip-fighting became an integral way of ensuring that an opponent could not get a firm hold to execute their own throw.

Grips had been something that had received scant attention from generations of *judoka*. They had been taught to take hold of the sleeve with their left hand and the collar with their right. In the 1950s, Kenshiro Abbe had a revolutionary idea of using a high collar grip that went round the back of an opponent's neck, all the better to control the head. Abbe was a very successful competitor, but his tactics were frowned upon by many traditionalists and no major consideration was given to alternative grips until the 1970s.

In 1975 Neil Adams, aged just 16, made his first trip to Japan to train and was horrified to find that because of the tactical gripping that was going on he was unable to gain any great success in *randori* against his Japanese fighting partners. Adams quickly took the lessons on board, but even so, two years later in the European Championships, he was defeated by the Russian Vladimir Nevzerov, whose understanding of mat craft was far superior to that of Adams.

Adams noted of a picture taken at the time that his kit had appeared "at least two sizes to big". It meant that while he struggled to gain a hold of the tightly fitted *gi* of Nevzerov, the Russian was able to control him through the looseness of his own kit. Adams responded by purchasing a tighter fitting *gi* and making a closer study of grip-fighting techniques.

Adams remained one of the most stylish fighters of his era, always preferring to do his judo standing erect, rather than crouching in the style of a wrestler or sambo player, yet he recognised that to succeed at the highest level he needed to master the art of dislodging an opponent's grip and securing his own against opponents that feared his ability once he had a hold of their jacket.

Judo kits had undergone changes before the 1970s. The kit is based on the traditional Japanese *kimono*, although in the early days the sleeves and trouser legs were cut considerably shorter than today. Kano had the sleeves lengthened to allow for what became the traditional grip, whereby the left hand could act as the pulling hand, the right, on the collar, as the direction hand. He had noted that the shorter sleeve allowed a certain amount of avoidance.

In the 1970s, judo players started to take advantage of the fact that the rules were vague on what could and could not be done with a kit. An excessively tight, or heavy kit makes it harder for an opponent to get any real purchase. Many top players had kits made to measure, with heavier cotton and even into the 21st century some judo collars are very hard to take a hold of.

In 1990 the IJF made an attempt to control the situation by issuing new rules regarding the jacket. The sleeve had to have a minimum reach to the fists and a space of 10 to 15 centimetres was required between the sleeve and the arm.

It was not the last word on jackets, however, as many continued to look into ways that they could manipulate the rules on both clothing and the way they could control their opponent through aggressive grip fighting.

It was, by now, a regular occurrence for rules to be changed. As well as spectator considerations, the authorities had to be continually aware of the sportsmanship that was being carried out as competitors looked for any advantage, however slight, they could get.

Another significant change took place in 1984 when *kani-basami* (flying scissors) was banned. This had been a very spectacular and well-liked technique for many, but was finally laid to rest after Yasuhiro Yamashita suffered a broken leg from it at the hands of his fierce rival Endo.

Many would argue that *kani-basami* was not, and is not, a particularly dangerous throw, the danger coming rather from *uki's* resistance to the backward force applied. Yet Yamashita was not the only high-profile judoka to suffer from it. In the 1970s the Hungarian Imre Vargra twice broke opponents' legs in high-level competition using the technique.

Banning such techniques from judo either for safety reasons, or to allow a contest to flow, was not new. However, the problem is that once any technique is removed from contest judo it tends to gets lost all together, because of the emphasis on *shiai*.

Such tactics as *ashi-garami* (knee entanglement or lock) and *dojimi* (trunk squeeze) were other techniques that Kano was

50

happy with originally, but had to cut from *randori* early on for safety reason. *Kawazu gake* (grapevine) is another technique that remains in the Kodokan's definitive book of techniques, but is strictly not allowed in contest or *randori*. Another judgement in the 1970s saw the removal of an *ippon* score for picking up an opponent who was lying on his back and raising him above shoulder height.

That latter technique was on its way out as a useful technique anyway, while the former was wholly frowned upon by most coaches. Certainly most rule changes in recent years have been to combat excessive mat craft. Rules have been introduced to stop tactical manoeuvres such as refusing to allow an opponent to take a hold. Other tactical ruses that have been outlawed include 'pistol gripping' whereby the end of an opponent's sleeve is held between the thumb and forefinger and 'cat gripping' a method of folding the opponent's sleeve within the grip.

While these rules are aimed at stopping spoiling tactics in contest, it is also true that such offending methods are also a block to judo being seen by a wider audience as entertaining - the impetus for rule changes in the latter part of the 20th century had more to do with judo as a spectator sport than anything else.

Those that trained at judo merely to win contests devised a number of tactics to gain an advantage and the rule-makers had to keep a continuing eye on developments. Resisting grips, time-wasting and other similar tactics had to be countered with rule changes.

It is widely recognised that the advent of judo as an Olympic sport was the watershed to many changes that the traditionalists despised. Intriguingly many, though by no means all, of these changes have not been transferred into the grading system. Weight categories are only loosely considered in most organisations when it comes to grading events and the lower scores of *koka* and *yuko* are not considered at all. This means that contest grading is fought in a very different manner. Rather than trying to merely win the bout, a *judoka* must impress the grading officer with his or her judo spirit. In turn, this means that it is pointless trying to gain an early minor advantage and then waste time.

One-to-one restraining method: *Kesegatame* was once favoured by the British police. Judo does not allow attacks to the face, kicks or punches in *randori*, but even with these conditions removed, *Kesegatame* remains a powerful way of holding down an assailant until help arrives.

Kanibasami. Now banned in contest as a dangerous technique.
The real danger comes from resistance to the throw.

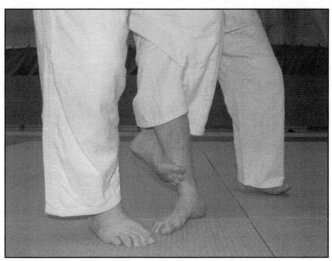

Kawazu-gake. Also known as a grapevine. On completion this
technique can snap a cruciate ligament as the author can testify,
having been on the receiving end in the late 1980s.
This is also an illegal contest technique.

53

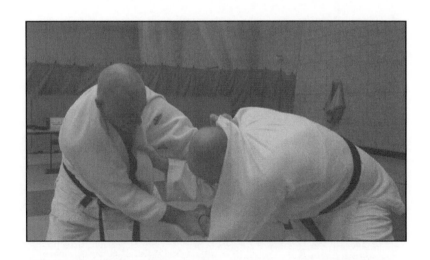

Grip fighting is an essential element of judo, but since the 1970s it has taken on a greater significance as judo categorically moved into the world of sport.

It was, perhaps, inevitable that with the ruling bodies opting to go down the route of sport, traditionalists would form breakaway organisations. There were certainly many traditionally-minded people that remained in the main body of judo organisations across the world, but increasingly their voices became lost under a welter of changes. Both organisationally and technically the main bodies were driven by the need for judo to remain an attraction to sponsors and Olympic-minded benefactors. Objectors had to be by-passed.

In Britain the main breakaway from the BJA came as early as the mid-1950s and was led by a Japanese of immense standing in the world of judo. There were other breakaways and indeed splinters from the breakaways, but the unrivalled traditional group was to become the British Judo Council, established by Abbe.

He was eventually joined by a stalwart of British judo in the shape of Masutaro Otani, who had been a resident of Britain for many years and a personal assistant to Yukio Tani, the former Budokwai head coach.

Abbe had been brought over to Britain at the expense of the London Society of Judo, but was quickly seen as a maverick. His style of judo was considerably different to that of the doyen of British judo, Koizumi, and there was possibly a level of tension between the two because Abbe, while much younger than Koizumi, was of a higher grade – he was as a 7th *dan* the highest graded Japanese *judoka* operating outside of Japan at the time.

When Abbe broke away from the BJA there were clear attempts by the parent organisation to smear his name. He was accused of being a drunkard who smoked incessantly and his teaching methods were called into question. Yet nobody could argue with his pedigree as a *judoka*, who was both very effective in contest, yet also an upholder of certain traditions. A former double All-Japan Champion, he had been the editor of the All Japan Judo organisation's official magazine and had trained a number of Japanese police judo clubs. His judo was of a quality which Europe had not previously seen and one that many believe has not been surpassed even now.

Abbe's BJC grew rapidly in the late 1950s and early 1960s and at about the same time the BJA suffered another breakaway with the formation of the Amateur Judo Association.

The various organisations could, perhaps, have happily co-existed but for judo's inclusion in the Olympics. In 1963 there was a three-way contest held between the BJA, BJC and AJA to decide who would have the right to organise Britain's Olympic team. Some seemed to think that the Association, who won the contest convincingly, should use its position of authority to select the best contest people from across the board, but in fact the BJA took their emphatic victory as a cue to establish themselves as the only official voice of judo in Britain.

Such an arrangement suited government and quasi-government bodies, since dealing with one national body is considerably easier than dealing with several. Judo as an Olympic sport was entitled to public funding and this was channelled through the Association.

There remained, however, a number of traditionalists, most notably within the Council, that continued to work within schools and adult education, teaching their brand of judo.

The Association's grip, however, tightened and over the years a certain amount of animosity developed and continued. That friction was not purely between the Association and outside bodies. Within their own organisation the Association had some senior members that cherished old judo principles and baulked at both the machinations and the style of judo that the younger element displayed.

The London School of Judo, run by Eric Dominy and George Chew, and originally an overflow of the Budokwai, eventually pulled out of organising competitions because of the emphasis that was being placed on medal winning. The club continued to send some of its members to outside contests and indeed they had notable successes, but fundamentally the club were opposed to the drift towards contest being the ultimate activity of judo.

Inevitably, as judo became more popular in Britain and Europe, a certain style of judo emerged that was distinct to that of the Japanese. Again, the process of evolution was not a smooth one and generally those that preferred the traditional methods of practicing judo were the same people who adhered to a holistic view of their activity.

There was nothing new in western and eastern ideas meeting and forming a synthesis. Even some of the Japanese masters who travelled across to Europe were keen to adapt their judo to suit their new audiences who by-and-large had different physical builds and mentalities. One of those was Mikonosuke Kawaishi, who became the technical director of the French Federation of Judo.

Kawaishi, a Kodokan 7th *dan* wrote in the forward of his book, *My Method of Judo*, in 1955: "Every nation possesses its own customs which characterise it, certain ways of living which are personal to it.

"Japan, for example, has some customs which differ greatly from those of European countries and it is in the bosom of this special Japanese environment that judo was born and has grown. Quite simply to implant this judo in Europe, to make it grow and prosper while following step-by-step the principles of Japanese instruction without transposing them, nor adapting them to the occidental mentality, was to expose them to grave miscalculation."

Yet Kawaishi was keen as well for people to understand it was the teaching method that required adjustment, not the art itself. He said: "It was not the judo which [is] at fault, nor the men who lacked natural aptitudes. It was the method of instruction which was not appropriate."

It was Kawaishi who introduced the colour belt system into judo, believing that it would act as an encouragement as western *judoka* struggled to go through their grades with no visible sign of their progress.

The fact that the argument between traditionalist and modernizers was not merely an east-west divide can be seen by the stand taken by Geesink regarding Kawaishi's modernisation. The Dutchman had hurt the Japanese with his World and Olympic victories, but he remained an adherent to traditional judo values and was not keen on the way that Kawaishi was trying to give judo a western feel.

Geesink was no reactionary. He was happy to move forward with the times, but also believed in the core values of Kano's judo, both as a system of contest and a broader activity for individual betterment. He recognised the work done by Kawaishi in popularising judo in Europe, not least through his introduction of the colour belt system, but suggested that in doing so had gone too far in trying to westernise the activity. He said: "People speak of Kano's judo and Kawaishi's judo. Kawaishi thought he had to throw Kano's principles overboard. He ignored the natural development in building principles and made new classifications. Moreover, he included throws which do not occur in Kano's principles."

Kawaishi did not see things this way. According to the man himself he was still keen that principles of judo, as laid down by Kano, were adhered to, but his was not the only voice seeking change. Others had fundamentally different views to both Kawaishi and the founder of judo. Kawaishi may have wanted to introduce a modernised grading system and indeed he was keen for some of the non-*randori* techniques of judo and *jujutsu* to be maintained, but others were looking at the core activities of *randori* and *shiai* with a view to major changes.

One such man, who had received tuition at the Kodokan but later disavowed almost completely the ethos and the technical side of traditional judo, was Englishman Geoff Gleeson.

He had been a special student at the Kodokan from 1952 to 1955 and on his return to Britain was the national team captain. A physically strong man, many felt he used this strength in a negative manner on the judo mat, something that is often regarded as a heinous crime. Nevertheless, he became the first British national coach in 1958.

One of Gleeson's main contentions was that traditional training methods were simply wrong for an athlete trying to reach the pinnacle of his chosen sport. If he had left this as a theory, he may have long been considered within the judo fraternity as a useful coach, but Gleeson, trying to make a name for himself, suggested that the entire training method of traditional Japanese judo was wrong. He further argued that techniques that had been tried and tested were often totally inappropriate for western judo exponents.

In 1970 a team trained by Gleeson issued a challenge to the Budokwai. The idea was to see whose methods were most effective. The Budokwai at that time were still committed to traditional judo methods and had a membership that boasted a large number of people who had travelled to Japan for their training. The Budokwai won the contest handsomely.

Nevertheless, western judo was moving inexorably away from its roots. In terms of techniques, training methods and overall attitude to the activity, there was now a distinct western style.

With judo becoming an Olympic sport, to a large degree its future was taken out of its own hands. It had not been long before when, the Budokwai and a few clubs aside, judo was mostly practised in small church halls, pub rooms and the like. Even Masutaro Otani, recognised as one of the greatest products of the Budokwai ran a club in a draughty hall with no heating. Run on a financial shoestring, the conditions of such clubs were seen as character-building for their members. Judoists thought little of glory, their activity being well away from the glare of publicity. Yet now there was the ideal of representative judo on a grand scale.

If the inclusion of judo into the Olympics was to be the arrival at the promised land for some, it turned out for others to be a wasteland. From its height in the 1950s and early 1960s, judo experienced a tapering off of activists. There was, of course, more than one reason for its gradual erosion. Wider changes in society accounted for the fact that with a greater number of car owners, for instance, there was a greater emphasis on family activities, the inclusion of a television in virtually every home and a sophisticated marketing of programmes meant that it was becoming more and more difficult to entice people into draughty halls for two hours of physical exertion.

For many, the real reason of the decline was the way that the activity at the top end had morphed into a pure combat sport. In the fast-moving 1970s the kicking and punching based arts seemed to youngsters more glamorous. Unencumbered by sporting considerations they could promote themselves as genuine martial arts, while judoists now had to struggle with opponents that were more interested in developing their mat craft than absorbing any wider ethos.

Inevitably, as things changed there were those that lamented the past. In 1996, Kevin Murphy, a well-respected judo man who had been involved with both the AJA and the BJC suggested that judo was a dying art. Putting the blame squarely at the feet of those that had changed contest rules, Murphy suggested that the spirit of judo was being sapped. He wrote: "Many judo clubs have closed down, unable to attract members, others have gone over to karate, so what happened?

"I believe they became disillusioned. In the 1960s changes from the old exciting traditional ways of judo started to take place. It became no longer offensive or indeed an offence to fight in *jigotai*. In the 1940s, 1950s and early 1960s the referee would penalise a fighter for persistent *jigotai*."

Somewhat disparagingly, Murphy suggested that the crouched position of modern western fighters was ruining good judo contests: "I sometimes wonder if many of today's fighters ever recognise their opponents when they have their shoes on, as they only ever seem to look at an opponent's feet. We were taught to look into an opponent's eyes or watch their shoulders, but then we had no *kokas* or *yukos* to worry about. Now it seems to be 'get a *koka*, hold onto it, get a medal'.

"I believe that until we get back to the traditional rules and etiquette, recapturing the exciting methods of yesteryear, judo will be the sole preserve of a few hard knockers, muscle bulging up to their eyeballs with grips of steel but sadly little understanding of Kano's eclectic system of 'The Gentle Way'."

The world of judo is not a hermetically sealed one and as much as the likes of Murphy complained about it, changes in society naturally impacted on the activity. One positive result of that was an increased recognition of women's judo. While women had been involved in judo from very early on, the idea of women competing did not take hold until a surprisingly late date. In fact the first European female championships did not take place until 1950 when Kawaishi refereed the event. Judo did not become an Olympic event for women until the Barcelona Games in 1992.

The person who had the greatest impact on British female judo is, without doubt, Roy Inman. He had been a member of the British national squad and in the 1970s was asked to coach the BJA female squad. No doubt the job entrusted to Inman was not seen as particularly important. Yet he put British women's judo firmly on the map, producing eight world champions.

60

Judo allows locks to most joints, but in free practice and contest it is only the elbow that can be locked. This is because pain kicks in before permanent damage can be done, allowing the recipient to 'tap out.'

Katagaruma is one of the more difficult techniques to master in the first set of the *nage-no-kata*. All 15 techniques in this *kata* are applicable to contest judo.

Judo can be a spectacular activity. *Tomeonage* is a technique much loved by children and film stunt men alike. It was also a preferred method for small Japanese policemen dealing with rampaging Allied servicemen in the aftermath of World War Two.

Inman appeared to have a sudden, Damascian type insight into precisely how judo works. Noting that a female's physique is different to a man's and that she cannot rely solely on power to finish her techniques, he worked on a greater level of precision for his female fighters. He was clearly innovative in his judo, yet his technical ideas were much closer to those of traditionalists than the likes of Gleeson, even if he was involved in the coaching of contest women.

Inman got his fighters to increase their fitness levels as well as making them work hard on accuracy, so that as contests dragged on they would be able to despatch their opponents even if they did not have the physical strength to finish off a technique the way a man could.

It was a wonderful irony missed by many that Inman, in taking the challenge of coaching a new breed of fighter, was resorting to original ideas – that judo was not about brute strength and weight, but more about the science of fighting. The truism that 'a good big one will always beat a good little one' remained, but the boundary is always difficult to find and in searching out that boundary, smaller competitors can have dramatic success. Inman's squads were recognised not only for their medal-winning success but for the style of judo that they displayed.

Britain's first ever World Champion was June Bridge, originally a BJC member, who won the title in 1980.

In his early days as the British women's coach, Inman struggled for funding, but as an Olympic sport judo generally was gaining access to previously unimagined amounts of money.

Financial assistance from government and quasi-government bodies enabled those with ambition to train in more comfortable surroundings and with training being geared towards specific contests rather than being an ever-evolving process with no end, the tempo was changed. Judo was now, in the eyes of those who received funding, clearly and completely a sport.

Eventually Britain's time as the foremost champions of women's judo collapsed as Inman moved on. The Japanese were slow to consider their own invention as one that women could as should compete in, but when they did it was almost inevitable that they would produce some very stylish and effective fighters.

63

One of the rule changes that was evidently made for the benefit of those that saw judo as a sport above all else was the allowance of blue *judogi*.

Even as late as 1990, when new rules has been introduced to stop *gis* being tailored too tight, there continued to be a stipulation that the kit would be white or off-white and there was to be a limit on the badges that could be worn. Yet just seven years later those rules were changed again.

In itself the change could be seen of as a minor detail. But what it embodied was something that went way beyond a mere fashion statement. *Judogis* had gone through changes in the past. Trousers were originally much shorter, as we have seen, and the length of the sleeve has also changed. But these changes were to do with the way judo was performed. The introduction of the blue kit was about how judo was seen.

The man behind the introduction of blue judo suits was Korean Yong Sung Park, who was elected as president of the IJF in 1995. He was clearly interested in the future of judo as a world spectator sport, rather than as a martial art or activity for personal development and with that aim he established the project Judo Vision 2000. He spoke of "the importance of making judo a more attractive and popular sport to the general audience" and suggested that the blue kit was a key part of his strategy. "The viability of our sport [sic] . . . required a drastic change due to the increasing importance of television. This was accomplished through the blue *judogi*." An early supporter of coloured *gis* was Anton Geesink. It was a stance that did the Dutchman no favours in the way he was perceived by Japanese traditionalists who had come to terms with his World and Olympic victories.

The premise that television audiences would decide how judo was practiced had long-lasting effects even on those that had no intention of coaching judo to international competition level. A clear example of such a change was the amount of time allowed for techniques to develop in groundwork. As a spectacle, judo groundwork can be as bad as a rugby scrum: even those who understand what is going on have difficulty following the action from a distance. For those that have never competed, the action is simple not good or compelling viewing. In the interests of a spectator sport, therefore, the amount of time allowed in

64

groundwork before the referee calls competitors to their feet has been eroded. This has been partially responsible for the perception that judo is no longer an effective ground fighting system.

In 1997 the IJF once again revamped the rules for competing on the ground. Time in *osaekomi* had been altered on a number of occasions, the requirement for a hold down to score *ippon* being 30 seconds adopted in 1941. In 1997 that was reduced to 25 seconds for the simple reason that *osaekomi* was boring. That, of course, may be the case and once somebody is wrapped up in a good hold 25 seconds should give an indication of whether an escape is plausible or not, but to change the rules on the basis of what those that are watching think is a clear move away from the original purpose of the pursuit of judo. The time allowed to develop groundwork being equally reduced is not only indicative of what those that run judo think, but also more damaging since it allows a reduction in the skill levels of those that compete.

Thankfully, many clubs continue to allow their members to train in a manner in groundwork that does allow more time to develop a dominant position.

It is not just the time on the ground that has been allowed to slip, however. Because contests are now of a shorter duration, penalties have been introduced for passivity, which allows those that can't get past a predominately defensive fighter to simply let the referee penalise their adversary. This does not help them develop tactics against negativity themselves.

Judo was increasingly becoming big business. The Kodokan, still revered as the centre of the world of judo by many, was, in terms of leadership, being easily bypassed. The International Judo Federation was the lynch-pin of the sport, with the Olympic Committee being a guiding influence as well. The Kodokan continued its position of respect, but rather like a monarch within a democratic society its power had been neutered and finally usurped.

As the 20th century turned the corner into the 21st the IJF and the EJU were frequently at loggerheads on how they saw their activity managed. Park survived as president of the IJF against a European challenge, the result being disputed by those who accused Park of vote-rigging.

The dispute ran for some years, but in 2007 Park finally resigned his positions. His resignation sparked a flurry of behind-the-scenes activity, the upshot of which included the ousting of Yasuhiro Yamashita from the IJF education committee. Yamashita was a heavy casualty for the All Japan Judo Federation. His departure meant that for the first time since 1952, when they joined the IJF, Japan was without representation at the highest level of the organisation. Immediately there was speculation that long sought after changes would be made by the now European-dominated IJF, changes that the more traditionally minded Japanese had tried to block around etiquette, dress and point scoring.

The removal of Park and the installation of Austrian Marius Vizer as the new president meant that the way was clear for the Europeans to consider yet more far-reaching changes to the way judo is practiced and, perhaps more relevantly, viewed.

First up for consideration was the scoring system, which some considered outdated and overly fussy. Judgement calls by referees were becoming increasingly difficult and the amount of positive and negative scores left even experienced spectators unclear as to what might be unfolding in a contest.

In early 2008, therefore, it was suggested that the scores of *koka* and *wazari* be removed. The loss of the *koka* score would not cause any traditionalist to lose any sleep, but the idea of ditching *wazari* was met with horror. Those concerned with the image of the Olympic sport felt that there were too many grey areas in refereeing, or rather judgement calls by referees, while others simply pointed out that judo, as a fighting art, was a complex system that should not be watered down for the benefit of spectators.

Such was the turmoil that across the globe there were those that hoped the Japanese would cede from the IJF and, under the guidance of the Kodokan go it alone as a traditional judo organisation.

Yet with the international prestige that goes with membership of such bodies as the IJF and Olympic organisation such a move would have been brave indeed.

In Britain it rankled with the BJA that others wished to continue to study and practice judo outside their orbit. The BJA was recognised by government and world bodies as the national governing body. At various times it decreed that its members must not even train at clubs or with individuals that were not licensed by them. Its public face consistently put out the message that newcomers to judo should only train at a club under its jurisdiction.

This was, of course, difficult to enforce. For many brought up in a traditional setting, such petty politicking was unacceptable. However, as time went by, the continued propaganda, and increasing divergence of styles and attitudes between sport and traditional judo made the spilt became far more real than it had been when official policy.

In 1994, finding it increasingly difficult to access public funding, the BJC affiliated to the BJA and two years later was followed by the AJA.

Funding was not the only reason for affiliation of either outfit. On the face of it there was little reason for them to be directly involved with the BJA, but the wishes of some participants to compete at a high level, without having to drop their parent organisation, was also a factor.

Despite their adherence to a different set of principles, many *judoka* in those organisations wished to test themselves at the highest level. The only way this could be done was through the national governing body. Part of the idea of affiliation was that those wishing to go on to national representation and even Olympic-style and standard judo could do so without giving up membership of their parent organisation.

This dream of having BJC, or other non-BJA licence holders, reach such heights while remaining within the BJC was no more than wishful thinking. The BJA certainly welcomed others into their open competitions, but to train and be part of a BJA national squad, affiliation was not good enough. A full, individual BJA licence was required.

Jane Bridge had become Britain's first ever World Champion in 1980, but to reach that pinnacle she had been forced to disavow her membership of the BJC. Ray Stevens, another high-profile World, Olympic and Commonwealth competitor, was also originally schooled by the BJC and to this day retains an affection to, and relationship with, that organisation.

Martin Clarke, whose father, Nobby Clarke, was a former member of the BJC and founder member of BJC (Martial Arts Circle), went on to be a member of the BJA's Olympic squad in the late 1970s and early 1980s. Clarke was already a successful competitor in the smaller organisation but found it difficult to gain acceptance within the BJA.

Fighting in the heavyweight categories, Clarke felt that his strength lay in that for a big man he was fast, but on joining the elite BJA squad he was compelled to build up his strength, inevitably trading in his speed as he did so. He also felt that his style was cramped by the methods used within the BJA.

Ultimately Clarke did not realise his dream of reaching the Olympics, but on moving away from the BJA he did win a World Masters medal in 2001.

In reality, the affiliations of the BJC and the AJA often did not work. Clubs trying to access public funding still had to affiliate to the BJA individually and those that wished to progress their fighting careers were forced to hold specific BJA licences. In the meantime, the BJA continued to receive 15 per cent of the total membership subscriptions of the BJC and 10 per cent of the AJA's headquarters income.

With affiliation, the BJA lifted its ban on members training with non-BJA clubs and those with BJC and AJA licences were allowed to contest in BJA events. There remained a guarded attitude to those not affiliated, however. This situation was not necessarily one to which those outside the mainstream objected.

Left to their own devices, many were quite glad to have nothing to do with sport judo and its governing body. Organisations such as *Seishin Budo*, established by Alan Fromm, a former BJC member and the Universal *Budo* Association run by another former BJC man John Goldman, were happy to plough their own furrow. Both organisations had levels of success locally even if they could not compete with the bigger organisations in terms of national recruitment.

Neither had the desire to seek out and promote champions of judo, but were more interested in promoting the traditional values of judo. For these and other organisations the emphasis on contest judo was unpalatable. There was, they believed, a genuinely unbridgeable divide between what they promoted and what was happening at a national level.

In fact many of the splinter groups from the BJC were formed by those that felt the BJC were moving too close to the BJA.

For its part the BJA was unhappy that others wished to train at judo outside their orbit. Yet the numbers of people training at judo independently of the BJA remained high. In 2008 it was estimated that there were in the region of 40,000 people practicing judo in Britain with the BJA only accounting for half of them. Clearly then, even when not marketed nationally or cohesively, there continues to be a call for a style of judo that does not embrace the narrow Olympic-oriented combat sport.

Yet the affiliation of the BJC and the AJA to the BJA continues, as do the disputes. In the early part of the 21st century the BJA, with an eye on membership figures, tried to get the BJC to completely merge itself with the 'parent' body. This approach was unsurprisingly rebuffed, although there were those within the BJC that continued to work for a closer relationship with the BJA.

If the BJA did not offer a carrot to the BJC for merger, they were certainly capable of wielding a big stick. Accused by many of having a high-handed approach, the BJA were keen to ensure that coaching qualifications handed out by the United Kingdom coaching authority came directly through them. Attempts to get the BJA as the only body authorised to oversee the award were met with shock not only by the BJC, but by the many smaller organisations that saw an attempt by the BJA to take over the running of all judo in Britain.

This move remains potentially very damaging to the BJC and others. If the BJA become the only organisation to oversee such coaching qualifications it could price many individual non-BJA practitioners out of the market, forcing them to either switch their allegiance or give up judo all together. Some would feel quite happy not to gain the qualifications, but that would deter them from gaining access to facilities such as local government sports halls. It would inevitably challenge their basic ability to run clubs. For many, this was seen as the real purpose of this idea.

Smaller organisations are seen as 'maverick' and their grading systems disparaged. They are considered by those in the bigger organisations to be loose and dangerous cannons. It is a misleading and simplistic argument to suggest those outside the BJA are all rogues not worth their grades and unable to teach competently. It would be interesting to check the insurance statistics to know just how many injury claims are made by these smaller outfits compared to those coming from the sports minded clubs.

Scott McCarthy, the chief executive of the BJA initially insisted that the qualification should be used to ensure that all judo practiced in Britain should come under the auspices of his own organisation. As a non-judoka, McCarthy may not appreciate the many-faceted aspect of judo, nor the idea that those who chose to practice the art outside the jurisdiction of the 'national governing body' were often as highly educated in judo and as proficient as those that were in it.

Under pressure, McCarthy eventually conceded that the BJA had no natural right to vet and control all those who practice and teach judo within Britain.

While the BJA can afford to subsidise its coaches because of its relationship with the government and Olympic bodies, the BJC remains an amateur organisation with a budget that would not support coaching courses to anywhere near the same degree as the BJA.

The BJC coaching courses are hinged on the teachings of Akinori Hosaka, a Kodokan 8th *dan*. Hosaka arrived in Britain in the early 1960s paid for by a BJA club based in the Manchester region. A respected fighter, then holding a 4th *dan*, he was to become part of the national coaching establishment of the BJA. Hosaka and the BJA eventually parted ways, however, and the Japanese distanced himself from judo for a period before resurfacing with the BJC.

As the highest graded Kodokan man resident in Britain, Hosaka sees his role as one of trying to right the coaching wrongs of British judo. Basing his ideas around Ippon judo he eschews drop techniques, teaching instead that judoists should retain control of their own bodies in an upright position while despatching their adversaries.

To many Hosaka's voice is one of irrelevance, but his grade within Kodokan judo means that he should be listened to. While British judo, through the BJA, ploughs its own furrow, Hosaka is

keen that judo is returned, if not politically to the Kodokan, then at least to the principles and style of judo promoted by the inventor of the art. Interestingly, Hosaka's perspective regarding drop-knee techniques found an unlikely supporter in the form of the newly appointed BJA technical officer, the Russian Andrew Moshanov. Moshanov moved to have drop techniques taken out of junior judo in Britain alongside a general re-education of British coaches towards a more traditional style of teaching.

The Russian was never going to have an easy task of realigning the BJA, however. Many of the coaches struggled conceptually with what Moshanov was trying to do. For many years they had taught quick-result techniques, so that their pupils could enter contests as soon as possible. Now they were being advised to go back to teaching basic judo skills that could be used as a building block to contest techniques: the horse was finally being put back in front of the cart.

As we settle into the 21st century there is a fashion for the grappling arts once again, yet while many serious practitioners of these arts recognise the debt their own skills owe to basic judo, to a wider audience it appears that somehow such skills as those displayed within Brazilian *Jujutsu* are superior to the art that spawned it. It is an interesting concept, but nevertheless flawed. Very few, if any, techniques within the pantheon of Brazilian *Jujutsu* have not already been part of judo. Even the leg-locks are part of what the originator of judo envisaged as part of his art. Certainly striking techniques both from a standing position and from the ground have an early judo history.

What has made mixed martial arts popular has been the television coverage given to American-promoted events that pitch fighters from different schools against each other. Those that compete in the events quickly recognised the advantage that judo skills give in such a free-for-all contest. Take downs, and submission techniques taking straight from judo have been popular even for fighters not fully schooled in judo. It is a situation that would not have pleased Kano. The fights are base, brutal and glorified. Despite the modern glitz, razzamatazz and inevitable money that is attached to them they are in reality a throw back to the days of music hall prize fights, an echo of the activities engaged in by the likes of Maeda and Tani. It would be

Defence against a knife attack: The author seen here demonstrating the *goshin jutsu* as part of a martial arts demonstration in Edinburgh, 2005.

difficult not to admire the fighting skills on display, but the activity clearly does not fit into any Kano-like ideal of creating rounded citizens. There is and always will be something distasteful in naked violence being used for entertainment.

There is no doubt that judo has progressed hugely since its inception. Whether that progression is positive or not is a matter for debate. Despite the perspective of ultra-conservatives it is even legitimate to suggest that the activity is right to have moved off the trajectory suggested by the founder: nobody now would argue that those who formed the Rugby Football Union as an alternative to the form of football organised by the Football Association, establishing 'rugger' in the process were wrong. The development of low scores, penalties for passivity and the blue *judogi* are all logical extensions of judo as it was westernised and turned into a sport within an industrial and capitalist setting.

Development of techniques that Kano did not promulgate cannot necessarily be seen as retrograde, either. Kano himself pillaged ideas from not just other oriental martial arts, but from western-style wrestling too. Plagiarism in this context is not only not a crime, but is often the product of an open mind.

Kano would have delighted in the fact that judo has so many facets to celebrate. It would be a safe bet, however, that what he would object to quite categorically is the triumphalist and egotistical manner with which many sportsmen go about their activities. As someone who was a patriotic Japanese, he also shunned the nationalism that arrives, often uninvited, at the door of international sport.

In establishing Kodokan judo, Kano was very insistent on the fact that the activity should be a means of making individuals more socially aware, more rounded citizens ready to take part in a society that was rapidly trying to absorb a variety of cultural influences. Every judo coach should follow that lead and teach a set of values as well as fighting skills to those in their charge.

Appendix: Biographies of key judo people

Dr Jigoro Kano
(28 October 1860 to 4 May 1938)

Jigoro Kano was born to a wealthy family on 28 October 1860. At the age of nine his mother died and a year later his father took him to Tokyo, where he was educated with private lessons.

He was taught both English and German and later, whilst devising his Kodokan judo he kept his notes in English. It is said that he did this for reasons of security. While still at college he started his jujutsu training under the tutelage of Hachinotsuke Fukuda. At the age of 19 he gave a display of Fukuda's jujutsu to the visiting American President Ulysses S. Grant.

In 1882, aged just 22, Kano graduated to become lecturer in political science at economics. It was also this year that he established his own institutions: the Kobunkan English Language School and the Kodokan Judo Institute.

Kano graduated from Tokyo Imperial University in 1881 and by 1885 became a .professor. By then judo was already establishing itself as the ultimate combat art in Japan. That year Tokyo Police appointed two of Kano's pupils as their unarmed combat instructors.

Kano's influence on Japanese culture can justly be described as immense. Not only did he bequeath judo, but he was a tireless worker for the Education Ministry as well as a champion of sport within the country. A meticulous man he was both well travelled and erudite and was happy to absorb lessons from other countries to apply them to Japan.

He was a patriotic Japanese, but was also unquestionably an internationalist. He opposed the build up to the Pacific War and was keen to maintain good links with America and Europe. He believed that judo was a way of bringing people together from across the continents. Kano attended the famous 1936 Olympic Games in Berlin on behalf of the Asian Olympic Committee and it is notable from photographs taken at the time that Kano refused to offer the Nazi salute. When the German national anthem was played he merely removed his hat.

As an instructor Kano was both strict, yet understanding. He expected total commitment and loyalty from his students, but in return did his utmost to progress their careers.

His vision for judo included not just the *randori* that is at the core of most judo activity. He incorporated techniques from a number of other arts and was also keen to see kendo and aikido type activities included in the curriculum of judo.

Kano died on a return sea voyage from Cairo in 1938. He was returning from a meeting that had secured the 1940 Olympic Games for Japan. Some conspiracy theorists believe that Kano was murdered because of his opposition to Japanese imperialism, but there is no evidence for this. His body was buried at sea.

Mitsuyo Maeda
(18 November 1878 to 28 November 1941)

Maeda wanted to be a sumo wrestler when he was younger, but did not attain the required build. He remained a physically small man, but nevertheless went on to create history by, in effect, founding Brazilian Jujutsu.

Maeda took up judo in 1895 and on entering the Kodokan immediately took the eye of Kano. Kano assigned Maeda to Tsunedro Tomita, the smaller of Kano's top three or four instructors and it was clear that Maeda was to be groomed to be one of the leading lights of the Kodokan – the next generation. It was not to be, however.

After the success of Yoshiki Yamashita in America, Maeda was asked to accompany Tomita to the states in 1904.

At that time Maeda was a 4th *dan* and the pair had mixed success. They parted ways a year late when Maeda started to associate with a Japanese professional wrester. It was, as far as the Kodokan was concerned, a slippery slope.

In moving into the professional fight scene Maeda had notable success when combatants were wearing jackets, but had mixed results otherwise. Nevertheless, taking a leaf out of the book of his mentor, Tomita, he persevered, going on tours of Britain and Europe. It was on one of these excursions that he picked up the name 'Conde Koma,' Spanish for Count Combat.

In 1912 he was promoted to 5th *dan* by the Kodokan, but there was stiff opposition to this because of his insistence on fighting in music halls.

Two years later he settled in Brazil, where in 1917 he started to coach Carlo Gracie. The rest, as they say, is history.

In fact, Maeda saw his judo as a fighting art and little else. He pared judo down to the basics of what he thought was fighting effectiveness. His preference for groundwork was partially because of the time that he had been in the Kodokan, when newaza was predominant, but also partially because on the music hall circuit he came across a number of boxers and found that they did not cope well on the ground. He thus worked on takedowns.

Yoshiaki Yamashita
(16 February 1865 to 26 October 1935)

Yamashita was one of Kano's early and most successful students. More than a student, in fact, Yamashita was one of the three early pupils that helped define Kodokan judo, alongside Saigo and Tsunejiro Tomita. Like those two, Yamashita was part of the Kodokan team that defeated all-comers in the 1885 police challenge competition and it was Yamashita that took on the role of Chief Instructor to the Tokyo Police.

Prior to joining the Kodokan, Yamashita was another who had studied *tensin shin'yo ryu* and *yoshin ryu jujutsu* and as a consequence quickly rose up the judo ranks. Like his mentor, Kano, he was fully committed to judo as a moral training. "Always try to think of improving. There is no end in learning judo," he said.

In 1903 Yamashita travelled to America to teach judo. It was during his time there that he famously taught the American President, Theodore Roosevelt judo. On his return, in 1906, he took part in the historic group that established the judo *katas.*

A formidable contest fighters, an exponent of *kata* and a gloriously gifted teacher, Yamashita was the first Kodokan Judo 10th *dan*. He was giving the award posthumously in 1935, but Kano dated the certificate two days prior to Yamashita's death.

76

Gunji Koizumi
(July 1885 to 15 April 1965)

The father of British judo, indeed the father of European judo; Koizumi was not originally a judo man, nor was he a judo emissary, as some mistakenly believe. Koizumi studied *kendo* and *tenshin shin'yo ryu jujutsu* before leaving Japan in 1906. An electrical engineer, he originally pitched up in the north of England, before moving on to America, where he taught *jujutsu*.

He returned to England, however, and settled in London, where he got involved in the antiques business, becoming something of an expert in Chinese lacquers. In this capacity he became a consultant for the Victoria and Albert Museum.

In 1917 he established the *Budokwai*, a society for the promotion of Japanese culture. When the club opened its first premises the following year, it taught *jujutsu*, *kendo*, poetry and other Japanese activities. The *Budokwai* was a gift from Koizumi to the British people and from the very beginning it was owned by its members and run by a committee.

Koizumi was always at one with the ethics of Dr Kano and in 1920 was happy for the *Budokwai* to take on Kodokan judo as its main activity. There was talk of the *Budokwai* becoming the London branch of the Kodokan, but this never materialised. In the meantime Koizumi, despite the physical distance between them became a close ally of Kano's. He was a tireless worker for the promotion of judo across Britain and on his death was posthumously promoted by the Kodokan to 8th *dan*.

In fact, Koizumi's death was sad. At the age of 80 he was still teaching judo, but on finishing a session on 14 April 1965 he commented that he wished "to see people think for themselves and not led like sheep." The following day he took his own life.

On the Chelsea Embankment there is a Japanese Cherry Tree, planted in commemoration of him.

Kyuzo Mifune
(21 April 1883 to 27 June 1965)

Mifune is considered to be the greatest exponent of judo ever. He got into the Kodokan by sheer stint of effort and against the wishes of his father, whom eventually cut off his allowance. A small man, he made up for his lack of stature in speed and agility, fully taking on Kano's premise that judo was a scientific art. His favourite techniques were a variation on *uki-otoshi*.

By the age of 20 Mifune was an instructor at the Kodokan. He did not, however, concentrate merely on teaching. He was a regular entrant to the annual Red and White contest at which he was never defeated.

His ability to perfect techniques and add variations earned him the nickname 'God of Judo.' In effect that is what he became on the death of the founder.

Mifune was promoted to 10th *dan* in 1945 and was responsible for heading up the Kodokan's tricky task of re-aligning itself and continuing its existence in the face of the American occupation of Japan. He did so brilliantly.

The promotion to 10th *dan* at such an early age was, in itself an indication of the standing that he had within the Kodokan. He was the second youngest man to receive the award and nobody has held it for so long – it was to be another 20 years before his death. In 1964 the Japanese Government awarded Mifune the Order of the Rising Sun. It is the only time they have thus honoured a man still alive.

Anton Geesink
(Born 6 April 1934)

Anton Geesink has probably had a greater impact on judo than any man outside of Japan. By winning the World title in 1961 he opened the way to weight categories being introduced and by winning the Olympic title in 1964 he opened out the sport of judo to the entire world. Later Geesink went on to serve on the Olympic Committee of his home nation, Holland. In 1987 he became a member of the International Olympic Committee. He came close to being removed over a scandal in 2002.

Geesink started his judo at the age of 14 and by the time he came to conqueror the world his huge frame gave him an undeniable edge against his smaller Japanese adversaries. Geesink, however, was happy to learn from the Japanese and his respect for Japanese culture and tradition within judo earned him the Order of Sacred Treasure from the Japanese government. This was a rare gift for a foreigner.

On retiring from contest judo in 1967, Geesink intended to continue his involvement in judo. He gained a Kodokan 7th *dan* and was seen as an ambassador for the sport, writing a number of books on judo. However, in 1975 he blotted his copybook by becoming involved in an early version of mixed martial arts contest, something that the Kodokan continued to frown upon. That involvement possibly cost him further promotion within the Kodokan, his later grades coming via the International Judo Federation. He remains the IJF's only 10th *dan*.

Kenshiro Abbe

(15 December 1915 to 1 December 1985)

Kenshiro Abbe was one of the most accomplished martial artists the world has ever known. Possibly, the most accomplished. Graded to 8th *dan* in both judo and *aikido*, he was also a senior grade in *kendo* and karate. It was Abbe that was responsible for introducing *aikido* into Britain, but for many, it was his judo that made Abbe stand out.

The son of a *kendo* instructor, he became the Butokukai's youngest ever 4th, 5th and 6th *dan*. He was just 23 years old when promoted to 6th *dan*. A double all Japan champion he was also considered an expert at kata. He was one of just two people to defeat the legendary Kamura in contest.

In 1955, at the invitation of the London Judo Society, Abbe arrived in Britain. He claimed his mission was "to spread international understanding by means of judo and help forget past misunderstandings. I will teach all I know without reserve."

Abbe parted ways with the British judo establishment because he felt that they did not understanding the spiritual aspect of judo and were interested only in contest judo. On establishing the British Judo Council, he quickly attracted a sizeable following and spent much of his time travelling the country, running courses and giving instruction.

His impact was such that he quickly gained adherents, including Masutaro Otani, who had been an instructor at the

Budokwai. After seeing Abbe for the first time Otani turned to his senior pupil and said "We do judo his way from now on".

Abbe's suffered serious injuries in a car accident and returned to Japan in 1964. His ability to train and teach judo had been severely affected, although he did return to Britain again later in the 1960s. He suffered a stroke and passed away back in Japan in 1985. It is said that he was not truly recognised within Japanese judo because his allegiance was not with the Kodokan, but the Butokukai. He remains a legend to *aikidoka* in both Britain and Japan, and many people follow his teachings.

Neil Adams
(Born 27 September 1958)

Neil Adams is unquestionably the most famous exponent of judo that Britain has produced. That claim is a reflection of how the sport of judo has been popularised, rather than any great input that Adams has made to the activity or indeed his ability. Nevertheless, it is also true that Adams was a stylish fighter who spent considerable time in Japan absorbing the ethics of judo as well as its mat craft and skills – something that he did not, of necessity, have to do.

He became Britain's first World Champion in 1981 and overall has been the nation's most successful judo competitor, winning a clutch of European, World and Olympic medals. He lost just one major contest by Ippon and was recognised the world over as a genuine expert in the art of arm-locks.

In fact, Adams' skills in close quarter fighting meant that as mixed martial arts became popular he was in constant demand to teach at the highest level, even having members of the Gracie family seek him out for advice. Adams said of them that they were likeable people, but "misdirected in their concepts".

He has shown an understanding of the efficacy of judo as a fighting art and helped change the opinion of Geoff Thomson by coaching the celebrity bouncer for a year. After finishing his fighting career in 1988, Adams wrote a number of judo books and took on various coaching roles. He is currently graded as a 7th *dan*, is the Welsh national squad coach and is highly regarded in Britain and across the globe, particularly in Japan and America.

Chronology

1882: Kano establishes his Kodokan school of judo.

1885: In January Kano's Kodokan people take on a number of other *jujutsu ryu* to establish who will teach unarmed combat to Tokyo Police. The Kodokan win comfortably and Yoshiaki Yamashita becomes the chief instructor to the force.

1887: Kano establishes the *ju-no-kata* and the *katame-no-kata*.

1893: Kano become Chief Inspector of school textbooks and becomes principal of Tokyo Teachers' Training College.

1895: The Dai Nippon Butokukai was opened in Kyoto. The DNBK had judo as one of its main martial activities and the instructors were usually Kodokan trained, the most famous being Hajimi Isogai, who became a 10th *dan* in 1937.

1899: The Japanese Army opens its first judo school

1900: Two new establishments are opened: the Kodokan Black Belt Association and the Kodokan Research Institute. Kano's second son, Risei, is born. Risei went on to become the third head of the Kodokan.

1903: The first ever Kodokan 6th *dan* awarded – to Takefu Hirose and Takejiro Yuasa.

1914: The first High School Judo Championships are contested.

1915: The first Red versus White contest is established at the Kodokan.

1917: Kodokan 2nd *dan* Vasili Oshchepkov helps devise sambo wrestling to be used by the Soviet Union secret police.

1918: The *Budokwai* opens its first dojo in Grosvenor Place, London.

1920: Kano visits London and confers Kodokan gradings on Koizumi and Tani.

1925: The Kodokan opens a women's section.

1928: *Bojutsu* training instigated at the Kodokan.

1931: The All Japan Championships are inaugurated.

1932: Kodokan opens medical research section.

1935: Yamashita becomes the first every Kodokan 10th *dan*.

1938: Kano dies of pneumonia onboard ship returning to Japan.

1945: the DNBK closed by Supreme Allied Command.

1948: The British Judo Association is formed, as is the European Judo Union.

1951: The International Judo Federation is formed.

1952: Japan joins the IJF.

1955: Kenshiro Abbe arrives in England at the invitation of the London Judo Society. He breaks away from the BJA and forms the British Judo Council.

1956: First ever World Championships held in Japan. A team travels from Britain to take part.

Pat Butler forms the Amateur Judo Association.

1961: Anton Geesink becomes the first non-Japanese World Judo Champion.

1963: A contest between the BJA, BJC and AJA results in conclusive victory for the BJA, giving them authority to establish a squad for the 1964 Olympics.

1964: Judo becomes an Olympic sport. Anton Geesink is the only non-Japanese to take a gold medal.

1974: minor scores of *koka* and *yuko* introduced.

1980: Britain gains their first World Judo title, Jane Bridge picking up the accolade.

1994: The BJC affiliate to the BJA.

1997: The IJF promote Anton Geesink to 10th *dan*.

Bibliography

Books

Basketball, Collins Gem, Jeff Fletcher, 1999
Three Budo Masters, John Stevens, Kodansha International, 1995
Grips, Neil Adams, Ippon, 1990
Judo – The Gentle Way, Alan Fromm & Nicolas Soames, Routledge, Kegan, Paul, 1982
The Father of Judo: A biography of Jigoro Kano, Brian N. Watson, Kodansha International, 2000
The Pyjama Game: A journey into Judo, Mark Law, Aurum, 2007
The A-Z of Judo, Syd Hoare, Ippon Books 1997
Kodokan Judo, Jigoro Kano, Kododansha, 1986
Mind over Muscle: writings from the founder of Judo, Jigoro Kano, compiled by Naoki Murata Kodansha, 2005
Go-kyo: Principles of Judo, Anton Geesink, Foulsham, 1967
Judo a Sport and A Way of Life, Michel Brousse and David Matsumoto, IJF, 1999
The Canon of Judo: Classic teachings on Principles and Techniques, Kyuzo Mifune, Kodansha, 2004 edition
Ki and the Way of the Martial Artist, by Kenji Tokitsu, Shambhala, 2003
My Method of Judo, M. Kawaishi, Foulsham, 1955
All About Judo, Geoff Gleeson, EP Publishing, 1975
Martin for Moscow, by Martin Clarke, self-published pamphlet

Papers and essays

An Essay on Improving in Judo, Katsuhiko Kashiwazaki, published in Judoka!, British Judo Council magazine, Issue 77, 2005
Journal of Combat Sport, February 2001. Article by Joseph R Svinth
Private papers, Bill Stopps
Judo is Dying, Kevin J. Murphy, published in Judoka!, Issue 40, 1998

Internet sources

http://www.batkd.com/JudoHistory/HistoryNine.htm (07/05)
http://www.armas-uk.com/aboutus.html (08/05)
www.bstkd.com/JudoHistory/HistorySeven.htm (6/05)
http://judoinfo.com/jhist3.htm (6/05)
www.bstkd.com/JudoHistory/HistorySeven.htm (6/05)
http://judoinfo.com/jhist3.htm (6/05)
http://ejmas.com/jcs.jcsart_svinth_1202.htm (12/05)

Contact details for judo organisations

The British Judo Association
Suite B, Loughborough Tech Park
Epinal Way, Loughborough, LE11 3GE.
web: www.britishjudo.org.uk

The British Judo Council
37 High Street, Stalhan, Norfolk, NE12 9AH
web: www.britishjudocouncil.org

The Kodokan Institute
1-16-30 Jasuga, Bunkyo-ku, Tokyo, 112-003, Japan.
web: www.kodokan.org

**For more sports books
from London League
Publications Ltd visit:**

www.llpshop.co.uk

**or write for a free
booklist to:
PO Box 10441,
London
E14 8WR**